I MAY BE WRONG

WRONG

BUT I DOUBT IT

I MAY BE WRONG

BUT I DOUBT IT

Charles Barkley

Edited and with an Introduction by

Michael Wilbon

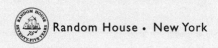 Random House • New York

Library of Congress Cataloging-in-Publication Data
Barkley, Charles.
    I may be wrong but I doubt it / Charles Barkley ;
edited and with an introduction by Michael Wilbon.
        p.   cm.
    ISBN 0-375-50883-X
    1. Barkley, Charles. 2. Basketball players–United
States–Biography. I. Wilbon, Michael. II. Title.

    GV884.B28 A29 2003
    796.323'092–dc21
    [B]

                                2002029169

Random House website address: www.atrandom.com
Printed in the United States of America on
acid-free paper
9 8 7 6 5 4 3

Book design by Mercedes Everett

Acknowledgments

I want to thank all of my family and friends who have
supported me and helped me to achieve great things.
I also want to thank my enemies for keeping me
motivated. I've had a wonderful life and I thank God
every day.

Contents

· Contents ·

Introduction
Michael Wilbon

The trouble is, the greatest athletes in these times usually aren't all that interested in expression, and the ones who have so much to say aren't the ones we want to hear. But Charles Barkley has always been both: compelling on the court and fascinating when holding court. Basketball has always been just the half of it with Barkley, which is why two years into athletic retirement he is still irresistible.

What professional athlete in the last twenty years participated more fully, peeled back all the layers, and loved it any more than Barkley? The games, the riches, the teammates, the foes, the confrontations, the adoration, the climb, the fall, the verbal sparring, the needling, the provoking, the joking, the challenging, the indulging; we can't imagine Barkley without all of it, all of the time.

We marveled when a man his height scored 40 points and grabbed 20 rebounds in a game. We laughed when he asked the devoutly religious A. C. Green, "If God's so good, how come he didn't give you a jump shot?" We cringed when he said an Angolan Olympic basketball player might have been carrying a spear. We wondered if he was serious when he said he would consider a career in politics, as a Republican. Usually, we were unaware when he stuffed wads of bills in the bag of a homeless woman in Spain, or gave a million bucks to his high school, or changed a stranger's tire, drove him home, then waited until the guy's kids arrived from school so they would believe it really was Charles Barkley who changed their daddy's tire.

Some folks loved it, some hated it when he said parents shouldn't depend on athletes to be their kids' role models. The folks at PETA (People for the Ethical Treatment of Animals) gritted their teeth when Barkley went on TV, eating an all-beef hamburger, and said the only thing animals were good for was eating and wearing.

He's never been one for political correctness. He has carried a gun for protection, but never run with a posse. During the Gulf War, when most of the players tended to keep their views to themselves, Barkley came to the NBA All-Star interview room wearing a cap that said, "Fuck Iraq." He is not for the easily offended, those stuck in neutral, and certainly those without a generous sense of humor.

One day last spring, while Barkley and I were talking for the purposes of writing this book, a woman walked into an upscale and very adult restaurant in the ultra-fashionable section of Atlanta known as Buckhead. With her were a dozen twelve- and thirteen-year-old girls, their heads newly coiffed and braided and teased to the tune of $50 a head from a group trip to the salon. As she greeted Barkley and told of her daughter's group birthday present, he said, "Whatever happened to Chuck E. Cheese? Ain't no Dairy Queens in Atlanta?" Everybody sitting within earshot smiled appreciatively, wishing they could have expressed exactly that, so casually and innocently but still right to the point. The woman blushed and said, "Oh, Charles," not the least offended that she had been the prop for a dead-on Barkley commentary on parental misjudgment. It was the perfect thing to say, and I don't know anyone else who would have said it.

Years ago, Michael Jordan observed that we all want to say the stuff Barkley says, but we don't dare. And particularly, most athletes don't dare. I don't enjoy going into locker rooms as much as I used to, not because there aren't plenty of smart and observant guys–there are. It's that guys with commentary in their souls are afraid to say what they're really thinking, particularly on sensitive issues. Sadly, it's understandable. The league might be offended, and if not the league then the shoe sponsor that is shelling out three mil a year or whatever it is for the athlete to *appeal* to customers, not potentially offend them. And if not the corporate sponsor, then the women or the gays or the blacks or the whites or the Hispanics or . . . *somebody*. And rather than take that public beating or risk losing that endorsement income, or sound like an uninformed fool, most guys just say the safe thing, or clam up altogether and put on headphones to shut out the noise of the world. I've never seen Barkley wearing headphones in public. Never.

Early on, Barkley made his peace with mixing it up, and decided the consequences were very much worth it to him. And that makes him as radically different in these modern celebrity times as a 6-foot-4-inch power forward. And most days it makes him a compelling figure in the world of sports and entertainment. When I was approached about editing his words I was excited because I knew from seventeen years of hanging around him that Barkley had things to say, things worth writing and hearing and debating, some of it about touchy and even volatile subjects of which most celebrities are deathly afraid. Not sound bites, not thirty-second commercial clips that have at times gotten him into swirling controversy, but fully developed thoughts he's been mulling and shaping for years. I may have edited this book, but it was written by Charles Barkley.

The first time I ever saw Charles was November 5, 1983, in Auburn, Alabama, on the campus. I was the beat writer covering college sports for the *Washington Post*, and I was there to see Maryland play Auburn in football. The football game would be memorable enough since Maryland was led by a young quarterback named Boomer Esiason and Auburn that day would unleash a third-string running back named Vincent (Bo) Jackson on the college football world.

But while I've covered football, I'm a basketball junkie. My friend, mentor and columnist colleague

Ken Denlinger–an even bigger basketball junkie–
made the trip as well. He knew the Auburn basketball
coach, Sonny Smith, and had arranged for us to go
watch the basketball team scrimmage that Saturday
morning before the football game.

College basketball was a regional pleasure back
then; you pretty much only watched the teams where
you lived. You didn't get to see North Carolina and
Duke if you lived in Chicago; you got DePaul and
Notre Dame and Marquette. ESPN was only about
three years old, so there was no Big Monday. There
also was never any Big West game starting at midnight Eastern Time. So I'd heard a little bit about
Charles Barkley, but I'd certainly never seen him play.

We went to the gym, and there was Barkley, 280
pounds or thereabouts, stuffed into those Daisy Duke
shorts that were still fashionable in the early 1980s. I
didn't want to say anything out loud to embarrass myself. So I just thought, "*That's* Barkley? This is the guy
people are raving about?" I was stunned. At a shade
under 6-foot-5, he wasn't much taller than me, and he
looked more like a defensive tackle than a basketball
player. But when the game started, he was a force of
nature, rebounding and leading the break and dunk-
ing. Bodies bounced off him. He played taller and
more confidently and with greater passion than any-

body on the court. A future NBA player named Chuck Person was on the court that day, but I don't remember anything about him. I just remember Barkley, and feeling like the handful of us at that scrimmage had discovered something delicious, some sweet new secret.

• • •

Every ballplayer who has come along since 1984 has wanted to be like Mike. Nobody wants to be like Charles for the simple reason that it's too hard, it's too physically exacting, too punishing. People fantasize about soaring over the competition; nobody dreams of the alternative, the hand-to-hand combat and mauling in the lane. For most of his career, Barkley was listed as 6-foot-6, which is nonsense. He's 6-foot-4¾ inches. That's at least eight inches shorter than Wilt Chamberlain, the only man to finish a professional basketball career with more points, rebounds and assists than Barkley. Barkley stands 10 inches shorter than Kareem Abdul-Jabbar, yet averaged more rebounds per season in the NBA. Barkley never picked on anybody his own size; usually it was 6-11 Kevin McHale, 6-11 Bill Laimbeer, 6-10 Karl Malone, 6-9 Charles Oakley, 6-10 Horace Grant, 6-10 Rick Mahorn, or 6-8 Buck Williams.

Over time, Barkley's shooting got better and his

range improved, as did his ball handling. But he lived for the mayhem within three feet of the basket, the elbows to the neck and knees to the kidneys, the slam dancing that allows the acrobats to soar unencumbered. Even at thirty-six years old, his back ravaged, he averaged 12.3 rebounds per game, still mastered this unglamorous but true measure of a man's determination and toughness. Appropriately, Barkley's playing career ended, for all practical purposes, with him blowing out his leg trying to block the shot of 6-10 Tyrone Hill. A scout who came back to an NBA general manager with the report that a 6-foot-5 guy could score 25 a night and grab 12 rebounds for 16 years would be fired summarily. Inch for inch, Barkley had to be the toughest and most resourceful sonofabitch to ever play in the NBA.

And the notion that his career is somehow flawed because he didn't lead a team to the championship is one I reject, the way I reject it about the great Ted Williams, who never won a World Series, the way I reject it about the fabulous Gale Sayers, who never even played in an NFL playoff game. Barkley's great sin was being born three days after Michael Jordan. He suffered the same bad timing as Patrick Ewing, Karl Malone, John Stockton and Reggie Miller: he was born at the wrong time. His fatal athletic flaw, if we accept such a notion, was not being Michael Jordan.

But it's doubtful anybody, Jordan included, has enjoyed himself more than Barkley. "Mr. Barkley, where would you like to sit?" often draws the answer, "Right here, at the bar will be fine." Any meal in public with Barkley—100 percent of the ones I've had with him—is interrupted by people wanting an autograph, a picture with him, a hug, a debate. The only time in sixteen years of postgame grub that I've ever seen him refuse an autograph is when some adult weasel is clearly trying to hoard signatures to sell. The well-known incident where an angry woman tore up his autograph and claimed Barkley was rude to her resulted from her asking him to sign for the seventh or eighth time.

Other than that, rarely if ever does anybody go away unhappy. Hell, people approach him with the intention of venting and go away smiling. Quick story: One night a few years back in a Phoenix restaurant, an ex-marine who was shorter than Barkley is wide and had had too much to drink decided he was going to start a fight. Why? His nuisance of a girlfriend had asked Barkley to pose with her for a picture. Real problem was, two or three of his buddies were poised to jump in. Charles looked at me and asked, "You ever been in a bar fight?" I told him no. He said, "Well, there's a first time for everything. Now, take off your glasses."

Perhaps sensing a sportswriter wasn't the ideal tag-team partner, Barkley did the prudent thing and simply charmed the drunken bums out of their rage and into a picture-taking frenzy. These are the kinds of encounters you risk when you travel with no body-guard (the NBA made him hire one at the end of his career but he's back to traveling solo), when you don't seek out the table in the booth in the back in the cor-ner in the dark, when you say hello to everybody, pick up the drink tab and tip the waiter too much.

After seeing Barkley need two hours to get through a basic lunch one day in Atlanta because of the inter-ruptions, a patron walked over, signed his name to a piece of paper, put it down in front of Barkley and said, "Charles, I just wanted to give you *my* auto-graph. I never knew exactly what to think about you until today."

Then again, it's the daily interaction with people that keeps Barkley in touch in a way most celebri-ties are not. The great attraction to him is that the same guy who said that an African Olympic opponent "probably hadn't eaten in five or six days" is the same guy who has loaned friends nearly a million bucks with little prospect of seeing any of it again.

I've always thought Barkley would make a wonderful talk show host, and he could be moving in that direction. Part of the reason, I hope, Charles wanted me involved with his project is he knows to a great extent we see the world the same way. We don't agree on everything. I'm a registered Democrat, for example. But we agree to the letter on the need for discussion on just about everything, the more uncomfortable the subject matter the more necessary the dialogue. If the discussion leader can be insightful, irreverent, profane and funny, all the while able to laugh at both himself and others, then it's so much better. Barkley wants us to examine our own opinions and make him reexamine his, and in the process we may all learn something. Folks are forever asking, "What's Charles Barkley really like?" Well, here's the best chance ever to really find out.

I MAY BE WRONG

BUT I DOUBT IT

What's Really on My Mind

I *May Be Wrong but I Doubt It* isn't a basketball book. It's not really even a sports book, although basketball and sports are the vehicles I'm using to generate a much broader discussion, and are the things I am most intimately familiar with. There's been increased criticism of athletes, sometimes by people in the news media and sometimes by activists, that we run away from dealing with serious social issues, like poverty, racism, politics and education.

Not only am I not running away from these discussions, at this point of my life—approaching forty years old and two years into retirement after a sixteen-year career in the NBA—I usually prefer them. I'm tired of talking about stuff that doesn't matter. I'm tired of "Charles, tell me which coaches you hated during your career," or "Charles, let's talk about which players in the league you don't like," or "Let's talk about groupies."

Most reporters, I can't even convince them to talk about any serious topics, which I'm happy to have the chance to do now. If the topic is groupies, guys will blow my phone up. That's easy. If I want to say something bad about anybody, reporters will hang on every word. That's easy. So don't turn the page thinking you're going to read about that, because that's not what this is. I've done enough of that for the last twenty years. What I've come to realize is that I can have some control over this process. I can talk about whatever the hell I want to talk about.

At this point in my life I'm trying to transition from sports into something broader, with wider social implications. I don't know if you can do it when you're playing. Guys get criticized for not being more socially conscious, for not spending more time talking about social issues, and that criticism may sound legitimate. But if you actually take on some social issues, particularly if you take some unpopular positions, you're going to get hammered.

People say all the time they want you to talk about social issues. But if you do, and if you take a position that doesn't go down easy, you're "militant." My favorite one is, "When is the last time Charles Barkley struggled? What does Barkley know about growing up poor?" Well, I do know. Damn, I was poor. I grew up in the projects in Leeds, Alabama.

If I was still poor, I wouldn't have the platform to speak up about the stuff we ought to be confronting. Some years ago, in a Nike commercial most people consider controversial, I suggested that athletes should not be primary role models. I told people to listen to their parents, not to athletes or celebrities, and I got killed for it. Is that bad advice, to say, "Listen to your parents, or your teachers, and not some damn celebrities"?

But that's okay. I'm not overly concerned about people disagreeing with me. I'm concerned with the response in that I want to get people talking, get the discussion started. I'm going to say what's on my mind. Dan Patrick of ESPN, who I like very much, introduced me once as "Charles Barkley, who makes you think, makes you mad, but sometimes doesn't think before he talks." And I said, "Hey, wait a minute. I know exactly what I'm saying. I may say something some people consider controversial or outrageous, but I've thought about it before I said it." I always know what I'm saying, and I'm always prepared for the reaction.

I may ask a dozen people about something, especially when it's a sensitive topic or something that's likely to be explosive. And I like getting input from smart people and people who've experienced things I'll never experience or haven't yet experienced. But ultimately I'm going to make up my mind and say what I really feel. Saying something just for the hell of it isn't worth anything because unless you provoke some conversation, what you're saying is irrelevant. Just because I say something and get a strong reaction or a negative reaction from somebody doesn't mean I didn't anticipate it. I don't like getting caught off guard. Hell, a lot of times I know exactly what's coming and I say it anyway because I feel it needs to be said, or I need to be confrontational on a certain issue. But I've thought about it, trust me.

And I also know people think, "Charles is just saying that to get attention." And, yes, there are times I'll say something crazy or silly because I'm not going to be serious all the damn time. And other times the way to make an important point is by using humor. But when you read my comments in interviews it's not like I was seeking attention. Somebody asked me to sit and talk about something. I didn't go to some publication or network and say, "Hey, I've got some shit to say." They called and asked me to talk about a number of issues. I've started telling people, "Don't ask me if you don't want to hear what's really on my mind, or what I feel is the truth about a subject." Is it okay to express myself only as long as I say what somebody hopes I'll say? Do you think I'm going to say something I don't feel, or just tell people something they want to hear?

In March of 2002 I did a piece for *Sports Illustrated* with the magazine's longtime basketball writer Jack McCallum, and immediately after it ran I must have had two hundred people come up to me and start to tell me their opinions, what they liked and didn't like. Some people who said they didn't even subscribe to *Sports Illustrated* said they picked up the issue and read the piece. Most of the media reaction to it had to do with my opinions about Augusta National changing the course, and why I thought they were targeting Tiger Woods. A lot of people come up and say they disagreed with what I said about Augusta National, but I haven't had anybody say to me they disliked the things I discussed in the piece. I would say to almost all of them, "Okay, you disagree with my view on Tiger and Augusta, that's cool. But what did you think of the entire article?" See, it wasn't as important for them to agree with me as to get whoever read it engaged in some sort of discussion or debate about the bigger picture.

I've been criticized for expressing certain views for nearly twenty years. And even though I never minded getting hammered, toward the end of my career I was thinking, "Let me finish my playing career before I start seriously discussing all the social issues of the day. I'll still be in the public spotlight because I'm probably going to be in TV to some extent. Then I'll be better able to handle it." The more serious the subject matter, the more time you need to spend thinking about it and the harder people come at you if they disagree. As I said, I don't have any problem with people who disagree with me because the real reason you take on serious issues is to get some dialogue started on difficult and sensitive topics. But disagreement and ridicule are not the same thing.

Another reason I'm looking at a transition is I don't know that you can give full attention to subjects as serious and as sensitive as race and the economy and education, then just shift into doing all sports. I don't know if the two go together. I've always contended that sports don't help black people. . . . We don't own any of the franchises, don't run any leagues, barely run any teams. You talk to these kids and all they want to talk about is sports, and I guess they don't realize how little other than playing sports black people have to do with the industry. But they all want to play sports. Playing sports is fine, but too often it's all they want to do.

Don't get me wrong, I love sports as much as anybody ever has, and I'll still be doing my work for Turner during the NBA season, which is a lot of fun. But my duties in Atlanta will be expanded to include appearing weekly as a special contributor and commentator on CNN's show *TalkBack Live*, as well as other CNN programming. And I'm going to take that very seriously because the show deals with serious subjects. The primary reason I turned down an opportunity at HBO is that it would have been exclusively sports. And it was a damn attractive situation. I would have worked on HBO's *Inside the NFL*—not with football analysis, because they have former NFL players and coaches who already do a great job of that, but doing interviews. I think I would have liked it.

But I need to transition because there are so many things people don't want to talk or think about, things

I think I can get them to think about. Most of the reporters who ask me questions are white; almost all are doing well financially. Most don't want to talk with me, a person they see involved only in the industry of sports, about issues that concern black and Hispanic and poor white people. I don't think they see that stuff as something they can sell their readers or viewers.

How is it possible that 80 percent or more of the NBA is black, and there are still so few black writers covering the league? How is that? How many black writers cover the NFL? It's still a handful from the conversations I've had with my friends in the media. It's a travesty. I know writers and broadcasters all over the country, and I know it's a more diverse group now than it's ever been, and that's really sad because it's still bad. I know a lot of white reporters who are real nice guys and very good at what they do. But many of them just don't care about this stuff and others don't get it. And when the reporter does care, I know for a fact sometimes the boss—the editor or producer or whoever—doesn't give a damn and figures the readers don't care. *"You think the people reading this sports section give a shit about poor-people issues? Man, you better bring me some stories where the coach is talking bad about the player or the player is talking bad about the coach."*

I pick up the very same publications and read columns or editorials criticizing guys for not talking about anything socially significant. And that's true of a lot of guys. But if you ask me, I'll talk about it. And if I don't say it, the guy isn't going anywhere else to hear anybody else talk about it. He's not going to the projects to hear it. The only time anybody white comes to the damn projects is to find a great player.

This is what annoys me about the whole issue surrounding Jim Brown and his criticism of me. I really believe Jim Brown is on the right track on most issues, and I like the way he confronts and deals with difficult stuff. But I think most of the mainstream press loves to hear two prominent black athletes attacking each other. They just love it. I like a lot of things about Jim. But what real substantive reason was there to interview Jim Brown in prison last spring, other than because so many of them knew he was going to say something negative, he was going to take the opportunity to bash Michael Jordan or Tiger Woods?

He's in there for problems of his own, namely aggression and lashing out. Does he talk about his own anger management? No. Did the interviewers who talked to him ask him about that? Apparently not. It seemed to be "What do you think about today's black athlete?" and he just started bashing guys, saying the same crap he's said for the last thirty years, and a lot of it is simply not true, or it was said without any knowledge of the people he's criticizing.

I don't want to hear from anybody that I'm afraid to speak up. But I'm not going to bash guys who don't. Some guys want to and can't, some don't feel they know enough, or they don't want to get ripped for taking a stand. I know this for a fact because when I do something like the role model commercial for Nike, or pose for the cover of *Sports Illustrated,* symbolically breaking out of chains, I'll start getting phone calls from brothers asking me, "Man, how's it going?" I say, "Sonofabitch, you know how it's going: I'm getting hammered." They say, "I feel you, I want to join you. I want to say something, but . . ."

I got some great advice once from Clarence Thomas: he told me to always try to control your message. So I've learned that. I know sometimes everybody wants to kill me, but that doesn't mean I'm going to give them the hammer to do it. I pick my battles. It's just that some of them, like racism and prejudice, are tough battles. Those are battles worth fighting.

Keeping It Real

When you're black and you become wealthy, or become successful to a degree that is still uncommon, you're trapped in a way. I remember the first time I heard Allen Iverson say, "I want to keep it real." Well, his real at this point is that he's one of the best professional basketball players in the world and a huge celebrity in America making $15 million to $20 million a year. That's keeping it real for him.

My "real" is no longer the existence of a little kid in Alabama growing up in the projects on welfare. My real is what I am today. That "keeping it real" shit is irrelevant, or ought to be. It's only relevant to the people who want you not to grow and experience new things in your life. So, if you achieve and become accomplished, you're caught in a trap. This definitely has to be a black thing, some garbage we put on each other. I wanted to keep up with all my old friends, because I don't want them to think I've changed. But you do change. You grow and you mature, and you don't want to do that same nonsense you used to do. I don't want to do the same stuff anymore. You're supposed to grow into new interests and into new relationships and friendships. I try to tell these guys now when they start talking about "keeping it real" that they're not some little "hood-rat" anymore, and I'm not some kid running around in the projects. You're a professional athlete who, most likely, went to college and put yourself in a whole new culture that is diverse racially and economically and socially.

You're now making somewhere between $1 million and $10 million a year and you ought to be trying to have a positive impact on something because you can. That's your reality. That's keeping it real now. If you're trying to act as if you're the same guy you were at sixteen, that's the furthest thing from keeping it real. That's keeping it phony, and it's total BS.

I'm nearly forty years old, have traveled all around the world, met presidents and kings. Damn, I met

Princess Diana, met Prince Albert of Monaco. So I'm not that same kid from the projects of Leeds, Alabama. If I'm that same guy now, all these years later with all this money and opportunities and mentors . . . If I haven't evolved as a person and taken advantage of these chances to say something and do something and help somebody, then I'd be a damn fool. I don't want to hear that shit about keeping it real. My reality is the body of work I've built over my life, the stuff I've accomplished.

"Keeping it real" sounds like an excuse. To me it sounds like the new way for my own people to tie me down and keep me from working toward something new. That whole notion had to come from somebody not doing anything, not accomplishing anything. They want to keep you right alongside them so you can take care of them.

You tell some of these guys you're trying to be successful and they say, "You're trying to be white." No, damn it, I'm trying to be successful. If a kid tries to go to college and improve his situation in life or his family's situation, we've got people saying, "He's a damn Uncle Tom." Man, this stuff is so sick it's mind-boggling. Even though it seems to be largely a black thing, I know we aren't the only culture that has that.

I was watching some documentary about life for Native Americans on reservations. And this one girl talked about being called "an apple" because they felt she was red on the outside, and white on the inside. She said it hurt her feelings, but it ultimately made her work harder to get away from that environment. The equivalent for black folks is being called an "Oreo," black on the outside but white inside. Stuff like that lets us know it does happen in other cultures, but I guess I just know of way too much of it happening in my own culture.

Black people ought to want other black people to be successful and work hard and accumulate some wealth and build a new damn reality.

Caretakers
of the Game

As great as Julius Erving was as a basketball player, he's always been an even greater man. He was such a wonderful guy, and such a complete professional. I remember being so damn nervous before my first day of camp when I joined the 76ers in 1984. I had called and asked my friends, "What do you think I should call Julius Erving? Do I just call him 'Doc' or 'Dr. J' or 'Mr. Erving'?" I was really nervous about it because, and you have to remember, this man was what you aspired to be, as a professional and as a man. At the start of the first practice he came over to me and said, "Hey, I'm Julius," and I breathed a sigh of relief. I'm lucky to have started my career in Philadelphia, where I could be influenced by him. One of the important things he taught me early on was to value the game. Doc put it so eloquently when he said, "We're all caretakers of the game." I don't want anybody to kill the golden goose. To be honest with you, the NBA is totally different from all other sporting entities because the people who produce the entertainment and the revenue and are caretakers of the game are overwhelmingly black. In what other sport is that the case?

To do what Julius said, to actually be a caretaker of the game, you absolutely have to play at a high level. Guys can do all the crazy stuff they want to on the side, but you've got to play. These kids now aren't the first to come along with personality. We had some characters back in my day, but those guys loved to play. World B. Free and those guys . . . they played, man. Bill Walton . . . Bill Walton had all that Grateful Dead hippie stuff going on, and you know that whole culture was way, way out there, but Bill Walton played ball. Even when Bill's body wasn't willing, if he could walk onto the court he laid it on the line. Larry Bird was a beer-drinking brother, but he brought it every single night. Kevin McHale, Robert Parish, Kareem,

Magic, James Worthy, Michael Cooper, Byron Scott, they brought it. It was an honor to play against those guys.

Bernard King brought it even when he had serious injuries. Micheal Ray Richardson. I tell you what, Micheal Ray Richardson might have been doing some drugs, but that boy was playing some ball, too. Guys sabotaging their careers ain't something new. Young guys don't realize they can't do anything that hasn't already been done. It's like I tell my younger brother. He tries to trick me or be slick and I have to tell him, "I probably have done it all and I've certainly seen it all, so I can't be fooled." I tell these young guys, you can't come up with any new stuff to fool me or any stuff I haven't seen, so I'm going to ask you to do one thing: appreciate the game and make it grow.

It's a huge responsibility for every single guy in the league. But it's an even bigger responsibility for the stars. It might not be exactly that way in baseball and football. But in the NBA, it all comes down to the stars, because stars get all the credit and all the blame. All those guys who were talking shit on a Tuesday night in December, you can't find 'em with the game on the line late in the season or in the playoffs. Remember that Indiana Pacers series against

New Jersey in Game 5 of the Eastern Conference playoffs last spring? There were a whole bunch of guys talking shit all week long, but in the last five minutes of the most important game of the series, it was Reggie Miller against Jason Kidd on every play. The only time other guys made a basket was off a pass from Reggie or Jason.

It's all about star power. You can have all the damn role players you want to, but if you don't have stars you're wasting your time. Hey, I think stars are the most underappreciated people in the world of sports. As great as Michael Jordan was, he was underappreciated, because he was able to be Michael Jordan every single night for thirteen years. Only the stars can do that. It's like being on Broadway; you don't pay $100 a seat to see the understudy or the costars. You go to see the stars. If you look at the NBA the last fifteen years . . . The Celtics lost Larry Bird after the '92 season and you couldn't look low enough in the standings to find their asses for ten years. The Suns haven't made it past the first round of the playoffs since I left in '96. Every team that has lost their stars went straight to the bottom. The 76ers didn't make the playoffs for eight years. How'd they get back? They drafted a star. Allen Iverson is a star. People wonder how the Lakers have been able to keep it at the highest level since Magic retired. It's no mystery. Jerry West was able to get Shaq and then he was able to foresee that Kobe would be a star. Look at the Seattle Mariners. They've got a great manager in Lou Piniella. He's a great manager of people; look at the guys he's lost over the last few years . . . all of 'em stars, too. Piniella is great, man. It takes a helluva manager to lose all those people and keep a team in contention. They've got all those terrific role players, but they're just not quite good enough to win the World Series.

I had a guy tell me recently that my high school had never made it to the state championship until I got there, my college had never made it to the NCAA Tournament until I got there, and the 76ers didn't make it to the NBA playoffs for eight years after I left. And the Suns haven't made it past the first round since I left.

We didn't win, but I know I was doing something right. But people don't appreciate stars. They take stars for granted. You know a guy is a star when people feel like "He's *supposed* to play great." The key thing is doing it every single night, being the guy the fans expect to do it, management expects to do it, and the other players on the team expect to do it. And the role players can do what they do because of the star player's presence.

Malik Rose on San Antonio is a really nice role player. You'd like to have him on your team, right? If he wasn't playing with Tim Duncan, people would be boxing *his ass out* instead of blocking out Duncan when there's a rebound. You see the difference? That's the way it is for a whole lot of guys. Role players never are guarded by the best defensive player on the other team.

In that context, Michael Jordan is underrated. Look at the levels of success those other guys had once they left him. When Horace Grant left and went to Orlando he helped them get to the championship, but the Bulls retooled the very next year without him. Being a star is hard, and so is the actual work involved to be great every night, and the responsibility. And you have to have incredible talent and a different mind-set to begin with.

Take Robert Horry. He's a great role player with the Lakers, and he was a great role player in Houston. But in between, he was traded to Phoenix where they wanted to make him a star. And he fought with the coaches and staff. And that doesn't mean Robert

Horry wasn't a good player, because he is. But you can't learn to be a star. You either are or you aren't. I heard Robert Horry say after he hit that three-point shot at the buzzer to win Game 4 of the Western Conference finals against Sacramento that one reason he's able to be so calm about taking those shots is that if he misses and his team loses, Shaq and Kobe are going to receive all the blame anyway, so why worry about it. See, Robert Horry understands the importance of stars in the league and how role players are supposed to feed off them. A star has to have extra toughness, that special sense of the moment. When everybody in the building knows you're going to get the ball on all the big possessions, that's athletic pressure. The pressure of being a star should be fun, even the part where you get all the credit or all the blame for what happens with your team.

The fans and the media may be fooled sometimes. They'll think somebody is a star, but he's not really up to the biggest moment. You can never fool the players. We know who's a star.

In high school I don't remember when I felt I'd become a really good player, and I don't remember a specific point in college either. But I do remember in the pros. I was in my room one night—we had just played the Knicks in Madison Square Garden, and I had put on a show. Rick Pitino was their coach, and it was the 1988–89 season. I was watching *SportsCenter* after the game when a reporter asked Rick, "Is it possible Barkley is getting to the point where he can take over a game like Magic, Michael and Larry Bird? Is he knocking on that door?" And Rick said, "If you saw what I've seen lately, he's kicking in the door." I'm sitting in my room, watching the 2:00 A.M. *SportsCenter* and I thought, "Damn, I can play with anybody in the world?" I sat there and thought about it for an hour or so. I went to bed, and the next morning I woke up and said, "You know what, Rick is right, I can play with anybody in the world." And from that point on, I just said, "There might be two or three guys as good as me but nobody's better than me." And that was the turning point for me; it came in my fifth year. Of course you need the talent to do it, but talent isn't the only ingredient. If you don't *feel* that way, if you don't think you're better than everybody else, you can't be better. People sitting at home listening to guys when they say that just figure, "He's too cocky." But it's absolutely necessary to have that attitude. When you realize it and can back it up, at that point you just have to get out of your own way.

The year I thought it would all come together was 1993, my first season in Phoenix. I thought we could beat Michael Jordan and the Bulls that year. But we had such a hard time getting to the Finals. We were the No. 1 seed, had the best record in the entire league, but lost the first two games at home to the Lakers. But we won Games 3 and 4 on the road in L.A., then came back and won Game 5 at home, in overtime. The next series was San Antonio, and I hit the shot at the buzzer to eliminate them in Game 6 and close out the HemisFair Arena. I was so nervous about getting to the Finals. We were up three games to two in the Western Conference finals against Seattle and got our asses kicked real good. I remember sitting on the plane coming back and everybody was scared shitless and nervous. People can talk all the shit they want to, but those deciding Game 5s in the first round and those Game 7s, you ain't eatin' and you ain't sleepin'. You're nervous and hyper. I remember walking around trying to cheer up guys and you could hear a pin drop. So I figured, this is useless, let me go and get some damn rest myself.

Frank Johnson came up to me and said, "Look, we're going to the Finals." I said, "Frank what do you mean?" And he said, "You've never been to the Finals.

We've got everything on the line in this one game. You play your best game, we're going to win." And I thought to myself, "He's right. If I play my best, the only other person who could beat us in the league right now is Michael Jordan. But nobody else in the Western Conference can beat us if I play my best, and we're going to the Finals." I got 44 points and 24 rebounds. Nip-and-tuck game all night, Eddie Johnson tried to bring them back in the fourth quarter, but we won and got to the Finals.

Then we lost the first two games at home.

The day of Game 5 in the 1993 NBA Finals in Chicago, I was pissed off. We had won Game 3, in Chicago, to make it a series again. But the Bulls were ahead, 3–1, after four games. Michael Eisner, or whoever was running Disney at the time, had called my agent. And my agent called me in the hotel on the day of Game 6 and said Disney wanted to do something different with its "I'm Going to Disneyland" MVP promotion. He said they wanted to hire me, win or lose, to look into the camera and say after the series, "I'm going to Disneyland" if we won, or "I'm *still* going to Disneyland" if we lost. I couldn't believe what I was hearing. I said, "You call that asshole back and tell him to kiss my ass, we're not going to lose tonight."

So I was ticked off all day. Then, I'm sitting there watching the news and they're boarding up the city of Chicago. The previous year when the Bulls beat Portland in the NBA Finals, there had been some rioting. People got out of control after the Bulls took Game 6 in Chicago to win the championship. And the storekeepers weren't going to have any more of that crap, I imagine. So I was already seeing dead-red because of Disney, and then to have all these damn public service announcements running on TV in Chicago about don't hurt the city and don't riot after the Bulls win tonight . . . I couldn't believe all that shit. So I started my campaign, "The Suns Will Save Chicago." And "Don't Let Chicago Burn."

I told the reporters before the game, "I love Chicago. It's a beautiful city, so I'm going to do my best to keep it from burning down." We won Game 5 to get the series back to Phoenix.

• • •

It's a wonderful life we have. Life is funny. Normal, everyday shit is funny. The guy who set off those pipe bombs a few months ago, said he's mad at the world. Kid is going to college, says he has a nice girlfriend he loves, is in a band and smokes a lot of pot. What the hell has he got to be mad about? He's mad?

I would get mad about stuff, but I wouldn't stay mad. Life is too short to stay upset and hold grudges. People are probably thinking, "Well, you got mad at the refs." But I didn't carry that stuff around. I will say, though, that I never got along with Mike Mathis. He threw me out of a game in Atlanta once. You know how you holler and scream and curse at each other? He threw me out of a game in Atlanta, then threw me out of, like, three more after that. It was never over. I actually called him to the NBA office in New York, that's how bad it got. We went up there and met with Rod Thorn, who was handling discipline for the league at the time. It was that bad. Mathis never let bygones be bygones.

The best one to me was Joey Crawford. Great official. Once an argument was over, it was over, which is all you ask. Mathis, once you've pissed him off you were done for the season with him, maybe your career. Steve Javie is good, but once you make him mad you're done for the game. Bob Delaney is a good official, too, but same thing—once you make him mad you're done for the game. Dick Bavetta is terrific. The late Earl Strom. Derrick Stafford is great. Problem is, some of these officials think they're the show.

People don't know how powerful these guys are,

how they impact the game. And league officials keep refs' fines and suspensions private. I never got mad when a guy said, "I think I might have missed that call." It's a fast-moving, difficult game to officiate. Most of 'em are good guys.

But I'm just glad I played basketball. Of all the professional sports, I think basketball is the most enjoyable. We play six months, then have six months' vacation. We don't do nearly the damage to our bodies that football and hockey players do. Baseball lasts forever. And basketball is the sport that seems to be evolving in a fascinating way. Look at the trend the NBA has right now with the international players.

Dirk Nowitzki from Germany, that kid can play. Hedo Turkoglu is a tough kid. They're not afraid of anything. Just look at the European players from a cultural and geographic standpoint. How many of those guys, particularly the ones from Croatia and Yugoslavia, grew up in the midst of war? Some, I know, grew up in or around it. You deal with war, why would anything in sports intimidate you? You look at Vlade Divac. The guy has had people in his life close enough to war that nothing on a basketball court is going to intimidate him. It's an interesting phenomenon. Shows you it ain't really got anything to do with what color a guy is, but how he grows up, where he grows up, the environment he's in. People try to talk white kids in America out of playing basketball, but that's just America. People talking about "White men can't jump" and all that crap. It's interesting, how all these foreign-born players are coming into the league now and doing really well. I'll bet you they don't have a bunch of people in their countries telling them they can't play because they're a certain color or race. It's a game that rewards all kinds of different skills, and it's exciting to see people from all over the world playing it at such a high level.

Nike took an all-star team to Germany one year, not too long ago. Dirk was eighteen, maybe nineteen years old. He laid a smooth 45 on us. He lit up Keith Van Horne, dropped about 20 on Scottie Pippen. He was quicker than Van Horne, and he took Scottie right down to the box. I went over to him after the game and told him, "I'll pay your way to Auburn myself." I was serious. He called me not long after and said, "I'm going to be drafted." I didn't know he'd be this damn good. I'm proud that basketball is producing great players in every corner of the world now. And I'm proud that I played twice on a team, the Dream Team, that had something to do with making basketball as popular all over the globe as it is today. I've had some of the great European players come up and tell me they were twelve years old when the Dream Team went to Barcelona.

My thing is, I want all these guys to do well. Basketball is important to me because it's given me everything in my life. I don't have my college degree. I don't know what I would have done otherwise. Basketball has been the thing that connects me with people in ways I could never dream of.

On game days, I could be in the worst mood imaginable–a really bad mood. But sometimes, I'd get a call from the Make-A-Wish Foundation–there would be people, sometimes kids, who wanted to meet me before they died. And the foundation would call on a game day and say, "There's a kid dying here whose last wish is to see you. Can you just come and see him?" I'd get there and sometimes the kid would be comatose. One day, a kid woke up for a split second and smiled at me. I was told he'd been hanging on. The mom and dad called me later and said, "I don't know what you did to him, but those few moments were wonderful." And I cried all the way to the game, just cried my eyes out.

Ultimately, I couldn't do that anymore on game

days. I was too emotional. I couldn't concentrate at all. I'd be wondering about that kid, whether there was something that could be done to comfort him.

It's very scary. It's uplifting, too, but so scary. Terminal illness is just . . . *man.* To think "I can brighten this kid's life, if only for a few minutes" is kind of overwhelming. And if you can't get some perspective from that, then you're hopeless. *I'm bitching because my breakfast is cold?*

Mom and Grandma

My grandmother has always been the rock of the family. She's really strong, assertive, aggressive. I've always been just like my grandmother, stubborn and strong-willed. I'm 100 percent like her. My grandmother was the father-figure in our family since my father wasn't there. She took charge of all the important situations, made the difficult decisions. She handled all the discipline. The funny thing is, my mother is just the opposite. She's really passive. My mother is overly sensitive and easily offended. Her personality is very, very different from mine and from my grandmother's. Because of that, whatever grandma said, that was it. It wasn't up for a vote. There was no debate. I don't know how many whippings I had. Let's just say they were numerous. My grandmother would use a switch to whip us, a stretch of Hot Wheels track, anything.

Grandma worked at a meat-packing factory, and it was hard work. Mom was a maid. There was nothing glamorous about it.

And we bootlegged. We sold alcohol. That's the way we made ends meet: selling alcohol. It was hard raising three young boys, with no husband and father. John is seven years younger than me, Darryl is four years younger. How much money can you make working in a meat-packing factory? Or working as a maid? So we sold alcohol. The house was like a casino on the weekend. Guys would come on Friday and drink and gamble until Sunday.

One of the fascinating things about growing up poor in those projects was that a guy who fit the description of being a bum, a guy who drank all the time and didn't amount to much, would most likely be protective of you. Back then, some of those guys who were drunks or bums would be the first to tell you, "Hey man, don't screw it up!" I don't think that's the case anymore. The culture has changed. But back then, the guys who didn't amount to anything were very supportive. They would go out of their way to keep you out of trouble. They knew full well which kids might have a chance to make something of their lives if they stayed out of trouble, if they stayed away from drinking and drugs and crime. They'd tell you, "No, we ain't havin' that; you're getting out of here. Put that alcohol down." It's true. They might have screwed up their lives, and some of it might have been beyond their control depending on how much education they had or what kind of job they could get. But they didn't want to see the cycle continue. I think a lot of those guys knew how difficult it was to turn your life around if you got started in the wrong direction. And they didn't want to see that hopelessness continue. That can be some depressing stuff. But at least they wanted you to do well. They didn't begrudge you the chance to make life better for yourself or your family. They didn't want to see you fail just because they failed.

It probably sounds strange for people who didn't grow up in those kinds of circumstances, but that's just how we lived. The sad thing is, in poor communities now, the drunks and addicts are the ones pulling kids down, not pushing them out. That's why I started going back to the neighborhood and spending time with kids. Derrick Stafford, the NBA referee and now one of my good friends, grew up in Atlanta, graduated from Morehouse. He once said to me, "I know how involved you are in charity work and how often you speak to kids at schools and camps and things. But have you spent much time with the kids in their neighborhoods?"

It was something I needed to hear because my view is that you can make it–that anybody can make it–if you just work hard enough. I tend to believe hard work can overcome almost anything. But now you've got thugs and drunks pulling kids down and these kids live year to year without any encouragement. There's nobody steering them away from trouble. In fact, somebody's bringing trouble right to them, handing it to 'em.

I realize now how much support I had from outsiders, but mostly from home. There were three important men in my life: my grandfather Simon Barkley, my grandmother's first husband, Adolphus Edwards, and her second husband, Frank Mickens. My father wasn't there, and I was always resentful about that. But I know how great it was to have those three men in my life. My grandfathers were spectacular. I was probably too immature to understand at the time how necessary they were to a kid's success. It's just so difficult to be successful without that kind of support network. That's why when I speak to kids, I tell them, "Hey, you think your parents are a pain in the ass now, but they're going to get smarter as you get older."

As I look back on it, I'm glad my grandmother didn't tolerate any foolishness when I was growing up. I believe in my heart there were other athletes who could have made it to the NBA from Leeds High School. Leeds was a sports factory in baseball, football and basketball. We were really good in all of those sports. But I think it helped me that I didn't know how good I was. Being a late bloomer worked to my advantage. I think it works to the advantage of a lot of kids not to be phenoms when they're really young. There were no AAU guys coming around, swelling my head with a whole lot of garbage about how good I was and how much money I could make. I had no letters about going to college on a basketball scholarship until my senior year. There was no Big Man on Campus attitude for me. My grandmother wouldn't have had any of that.

Anyway, my mother and grandmother made me

be in charge of my brothers by the time I was fourteen. They said, "You're the father figure. You've got to help take care of your brothers." And so I was the father figure. We didn't have the battles I know a lot of brothers had, because I needed to take care of them. With my mother and grandmother working the way they did, I was in charge of the housecleaning, too. That's probably why I'm a neat-freak to this day. Never did dishes, though. That's the one thing I didn't do.

I have a greater appreciation for my mother and grandmother the older I get because I realize they were willing to do whatever it took to provide us with things we needed even though money was so difficult to come by. I distinctly remember being the first kid in my neighborhood to have a pair of Chuck Taylors. Did you know that we get a new pair of basketball shoes every single game in the NBA? When I was fifteen, sixteen years old and playing basketball in high school, I would get one new pair of shoes every season. My mother would bring the shoes to the game, and after the game was over she came and waited at the locker room door, and I handed her the shoes and she took them back home. That's the way it went all year, too, because that one pair of basketball shoes had to last the whole season. There was no wearing them just to profile or hang out in. I couldn't wear them other than in a basketball game until the end of the season. She doesn't have to remind me of that time in my life because I'm constantly reminding myself. All I can say is "Wow!" That's why I said I can't imagine my life turning out any better than it has.

I never had any sense, though, that we were doing without. There were no luxuries, but we had everything we needed. The holidays were cool because the three of us knew our mother and grandmother were going to find a way to get you one really nice thing you really wanted. Now my daughter gets ten things. She gets stuff from people who aren't her family. Kids now get a roomful of things, and you have to wonder how appreciative they are because there's no sense on their part that these things were difficult to come by, that somebody had to sacrifice to get them.

My original professional goal was to make $10 million, play in the NBA for ten years, be set for life, and make life better for my mother and grandmother. Remember, when I was coming out of college I had led the SEC in rebounding, but I had only averaged 12 or 13 points a game over the three years I was at Auburn. As hard as they worked, my mother and grandmother saw every game I played in high school and I think they saw every game I played in college, which meant a great deal to me. They'd drive two hours to Auburn to make every game. Even in the NBA, they'd come to about five games a year. My grandmother actually thinks she's a coach. Kids won't tell you they like that or they care about it. In fact, I've never told them to this day. But I appreciated it. It meant more to me than I can probably ever explain to them.

I bought my mom a car, though I don't remember what kind. I bought it before I had even signed a deal with the 76ers. I bought my grandmother a car, I think it was a Lincoln Town Car. I think they've been through about four cars apiece since then. After the first one I bought my mother, she came to my room three times that night crying. I bought them both houses, and bought my brothers houses beside them.

The one thing I would change is that they still look at me as "Little Charles." It gets to be a problem when people—even your mother and grandmother—don't want to treat you as the person you are, but as the person they remember. But I'm grateful they've been there every step of the way and that they worked so hard and sacrificed so much.

"You're Always Saying Stuff That Inflames People"

Fighting prejudice is hard. Sometimes I just sit and try to figure out how it came to be in the first place. I don't have the solution to the problem of racism, because it appears to be a problem in every culture on the damn earth. But I do know where we have to start: by talking about our prejudiced and racist feelings. That's got to be the first step.

The hardest but most important thing is to get a dialogue going on racial issues. I think people want to do better, I really do. I just think they're afraid. They don't know exactly what to do. Nobody wants to make the first move. Guys figure they might get ostracized by their boys if they open up and talk about this stuff. I just try to create conversation because that's where I think we have to start. . . . People rarely talk about race until something tragic or ugly happens.

Once you have some violent situation, where a black person kills a white person, or a white person kills a black person, neither side can talk sensibly or rationally because everybody's already angry. You can't talk about it then; it's too late. When I get together with my white friends, Jewish or Asian friends, I bring up race when we're doing nothing more than sitting around drinking or sitting around having dinner. That's a good time for people to talk and see where everybody's coming from because it's not a conversation that's a reaction to something ugly.

But even then I get both white and black friends saying to me, "Charles, you're always saying stuff that inflames people." And I say, "Wait a minute. Why do you look at it as if I'm inflaming anybody?" They say, "Can't you do it in a nicer way?" And I say, "It's never worked in the last two hundred years with anybody approaching it in a nice way." There isn't anything nice about prejudice, is there? It's a catch-22. It isn't a nice subject, but if you address it you're inflaming folks. There's no comfortable or easy way to get at it.

Because if you accuse somebody of prejudice, you are saying they don't like somebody because of race or color. It's some serious shit.

People are so afraid to talk about it, they can't even get to the real issues, the difficult stuff that *should* make us uncomfortable. We can't get past worrying about disagreement, so we don't have enough meaningful conversations to make a difference. Damn, to me there's a lot worse than disagreeing with each other. What's worse, people hating and acting on that hate, or disagreeing?

Growing up in Alabama, race was always an issue. It's just different growing up black in Alabama. I noticed it, I felt it pretty much all the time. It wasn't something that people just put in a drawer somewhere. It was always out there, if not right up there on the surface, then just below the surface. You think I'm exaggerating? We had a black homecoming queen and a white homecoming queen. At the time, I'm not sure I even noticed or knew the significance of it. And this ain't ancient history. I graduated from high school in 1981. It's just the way it was at the time. But I never felt at peace with it until I went to Auburn. Once I was in a place with all kinds of different people and playing on teams with black kids and white kids and making friends with people different from myself, I looked back on where I came from and it was amazing to me.

I've told people that I found an environment with a lot less racial tension when I got to Auburn, and people have said to me, "Well, it was that way because you were a star athlete and you were treated differently." That could be true, but for whatever reason I was comfortable there. Out of 22,000 students, which is about the number Auburn had at the time, only a tiny percentage was black. But I felt good there, befriended people, had people of different races befriend me.

It was then that I realized that whites and blacks could not just coexist but get along and live comfortably together. Some people may not think that's much of a revelation, but growing up in Alabama you just always felt a certain racial tension. And I never had anything overtly bad happen to me, but there was just tension all the time. I felt it throughout high school, people not knowing how to act around somebody of a different race, people not knowing what to say, being afraid. Maybe it was because people didn't talk enough, didn't have any real conversation about what they were feeling or about what these differences really meant . . . if they meant anything at all.

How can you know each other when, in most places in Alabama—and definitely my hometown—blacks live on one side of town and whites live on another? We're talking separate lives. One of my best friends in high school, Joseph Mock, is white. When I think back on it, we didn't know anything about race early on. Kids don't know. And that's the thing about racism and prejudice that is really sick. As kids, we didn't know. We just hung out. My mother and my grandmother didn't allow any of that garbage. They told me, "Hey, boy, all white people are not bad." Between my mother, my grandmother and having Joseph as a close friend, I never bought into any of that hatred. Funny thing is, it's pretty obvious when two friends are of different races that they aren't natural enemies, even though we grew up in the midst of all that tension. We had to be taught that BS at some point. Put a little black kid and a little white kid in a room and all they're going to do, before their minds are polluted with a bunch of BS, is play with each other. That's all that's going to happen whether those two little kids are put in a room in Alabama or New York or wherever.

And to me, that's the proof of just how unnatural prejudice and racism are. It ain't something natural; you have to be taught it. How sick is that? You go from being naive as hell to having all this tension by the time you're a teenager. It's learned behavior, it ain't something you're born with. It just makes me sad, that ultimately people teach young people to dislike other people because of the color of their skin. And we do this generation after generation after generation. A lot of people reject that shit and they befriend who they want to and associate with who they want to and date who they want to. But everybody ain't that strong, to break away from the stuff they've been taught.

A whole lot of kids are brainwashed and get fanatical with the stuff they get from adults. You've got all these militia groups talking about being mad at the government. About what? Man, if black people aren't mad at the government for our condition, then who has the right to be mad at the government? What, these militia guys aren't getting a fair shake?

I don't want to make it sound like it's simple, because I know it's complex. Economics is involved. Poor white people and poor black people have been pitted against each other, even though they have more in common than not. A lot of rich white people will treat you fine, invite you to play golf, pay hardly any attention to race—either it's that or they don't want you to know how much they notice. But you go out to a bar with a redneck and he'll call you "nigger" in a minute, and mean it. I go to a bar in a redneck area down near where I'm from in Alabama and you can feel what I call "nigga-tension." Poor white people do that. To me, that's some seriously misdirected anger, because poor white people and poor black people just don't know how much they have in common. Rich people don't give a damn about either group.

But I'm not about to sit here and tell you I only experienced prejudice and racism in the south, although it did seem more in the open. I left Auburn after three years there and was drafted by the Philadelphia 76ers in June of 1984. Trust me, I've had plenty of episodes as an adult in northern cities. I got pulled over when I was behind the wheel of a Porsche in Philly once for what we call DWB–Driving While Black. People ask me all the time about growing up in Alabama, and no question there was racial tension all the time, but in certain parts of Philly sometimes you feel like you're being subjected to the Klan without the sheets. It's prejudice that's expressed in more subtle ways. You don't get hit over the head with it in the same way. And you don't find as many situations where people come right out and say what's really on their minds. For example, I thought much of the news media in Philly exhibited characteristics of racism.

I would be asked a question after a loss or in the middle of a bad stretch about the 76ers' chances of seriously contending that year or making a run in the playoffs. And I would say, "Our team isn't good enough," or "We've got to get better in certain areas if we're going to compete at the championship level." I guess I could have tiptoed around it and given some vanilla answer, but that's not me. And besides, I was asked a question and I was assessing the situation as I saw it. The headlines the next day would say, "BARKLEY BLASTS TEAMMATES!" But I'd read similar comments from Lenny Dykstra or Darren Daulton when the Phillies were in a similar situation. Those guys might make observations about their team that were really similar to what I said about my team. But the stories would say that Dykstra or Daulton was right, the team had to go out and get better players to get in position to win a championship.

What we were saying wasn't any different. In each case a leader on the team was making an assessment of what was necessary to win a championship. But I'd pick up the paper and say, "Damn, the spin on this makes it look totally different, when in reality we were pretty much saying the same thing about our teams." And after a while I had to say to myself, "Damn, there's going to be a double standard for me. This apparently is the way it's going to be all the time, that two guys—one white and one black—can make pretty much the same observation, but it's going to be perceived differently. They perceive that the white player is a team guy only concerned with team goals when he speaks up about what the team needs, but they perceive that the black player when he speaks up about the team's needs is a malcontent.

It's very subtle, and sometimes done in a very sophisticated way. I felt like, "Okay, I'm dealing with a much more sophisticated bigot here. No matter what I say, especially about complex issues, I'm going to be wrong, according to them." You feel that you're saying one thing, but they're hearing another. It's really frustrating, and it was a learning process, that's for sure. At first I said, "Okay, I can't say what I want to say because they'll rip me apart." I was going to deal with it that way. But, number one, that would have been taking the easy way out. And number two, once I realized most of the mainstream press was going to kill me either way, I adopted the philosophy that I'm just going to do it my way and they'll like me or dislike me based on my doing it the way I want to do it. I wanted to please everybody in the beginning and I couldn't. It doesn't work that way because you're going to get slammed. So I drew a line, decided to always tell the truth, be straightforward and say exactly what was on my mind, and damn the consequences.

Moses Malone's influence helped me figure out what was right for me, too. Moses is eight years older than me, and he was the first guy to come straight to the pros out of high school and have a Hall of Fame career. I really hated it when the Sixers traded him on draft day in 1986. He and Doc had led the team to a championship in 1983 over the Lakers, and Moses had been through it all, seen it all, understood what was needed to survive in the league and keep your sanity intact. He said, "Look, these folks aren't your friends in most cases. So stop trying to please everybody because you can't do it anyway." He and Doc were so different in a lot of ways, which was a great benefit to me because I could get great advice from two guys who sometimes saw the world differently. Doc wanted to please everybody. Doc is just one helluva nice man, and he had built a great life in Philly and had a near-perfect image, and I'm not about to say that's a bad thing. But Moses had the attitude of "To hell with y'all." And in the end, when they tried to trade Doc and they did trade Moses, it was obvious that no matter what you did and no matter how great a player you are, in the long run you're still just a piece of meat to them. It's a realization that you have to come to, that it's a hard business and people can make it harder with their own prejudices even if they don't know they're doing it. And here I was, a little kid from small-town Alabama, naive. I didn't know what the hell was happening to me and around me.

The real turning point for me was when I just got killed with criticism for answering a question on my own radio show. We were in camp–I think it was preceding the 1991–92 season–and we had one cut left to make before the start of the season, and it was coming down to Rickey Green, who is black, or Dave Hoppen, a white guy. And somebody asked me while we were on the air live who I thought the team was going to cut. I said I don't know who the guys who make that decision will keep. But some people might be offended by an all-black team.

I woke up the next day, and people were saying, "Charles Barkley said the 76ers will keep Hoppen because he's white." And that, of course, is not what I said. I still think some people would be offended by an all-black team today. I was asked a question, and just stated my opinion. You mean to tell me people think there haven't been times when white guys were kept as the eleventh or twelfth man so that it wouldn't be an all-black team? I remember when the Knicks had that all-black team and people called 'em "the Nigger-bockers." I remember how people around basketball, black guys and white guys, would joke about playing two brothers at home, three on the road, and four or five when you're trailing in the fourth quarter.

You think there wasn't some truth to that for some franchises at some points in time? I'm not saying it was that blatant in 1991, but don't tell me race played no factor at all in decisions like that. It reminds me of a conversation I had not too long ago with Warren Moon. He told me one day that people think race is no longer a factor in being an NFL quarterback. And while it's a helluva lot better with a lot of coaches starting black quarterbacks now, Warren pointed out that there aren't any third-string black quarterbacks. And that's a fascinating observation. You've got to be good enough to start, pretty much, to be black and play quarterback in the NFL. There are only a couple of second-string guys, but if you look at it they were all starters very recently and could be starters again. Now, tell me it's just a coincidence that there are no third-string black quarterbacks in the league? Twelfth man . . . third-string. Don't tell me this is so far-fetched, because it isn't.

Anyway, people all over town in Philly were just killing my ass. And I'm like, "Damn, this is all-out war now. I had no ill will in my heart when I answered that question." See, this is one of those places where being too uncomfortable to discuss the situation leads directly to misperceptions and hostility. If somebody wanted to open up a discussion about whether people are still offended by an all-black team, fine. In fact, it's probably a discussion we ought to have today. Seriously, just let people put their thoughts out there so we can all talk about it. We need to talk about issues like that.

But that hurt me to my heart, to have reporters who knew me misrepresent what I said. To turn that into "Charles doesn't like white people" was totally asinine and just plain wrong. It was mean. It bothered me to wake up the next morning to people calling me a racist, after all the shit I've been through down in Alabama. I grew up with my mother and grandmother telling me about the four little girls being killed in that

Birmingham church, about the marches and violence in Selma. That really bothered me.

There are times I may joke around and try to lighten the mood when the atmosphere is tense, but not when we're discussing a specific issue that needs to be talked about. That incident hurt me, and I just kind of laid down the gauntlet. I decided I was going to say what I felt about things, and if they are controversial or unpopular, then so be it. I wasn't going to become subservient and afraid to speak out about certain things. There might be a few folks who say they want you to speak your mind on certain issues, but most folks don't want to hear any opinion different from their own or the majority opinion because it's uncomfortable. It disturbs their comfort level. I guess the bottom line for me became "Screw it, I'm going to do my own thing."

Luckily, one of the few places where you don't find much of this shit is the locker room. Of course, guys who play sports have their prejudices, too. We all do. And there are exceptions, but when it comes time to bond together and form a team and play the games, players don't care what color you are if you can play. One of the reasons sports is so important is that one of the few times people forget about prejudice and bigotry–their own–is when they are dealing with sports or entertainment. They can leave whatever they're doing, go see a Spike Lee movie like *Do the Right Thing* and cheer like hell. Or go and see Michael Jordan play and cheer like hell, or Tiger. But away from sports or entertainment, their daughter better not bring a young brother home.

But the locker room is safe from most of that stuff because people care about winning so much. I guess it hasn't been that long since even great players were subjected to it, although I don't know how much of that stuff came from other players. We know what owners and general managers and athletic directors felt. Can you imagine Hall of Famers having been turned away from certain schools? Oscar Robertson wanted to go to IU, but guys like him and Bob Gibson got turned away from big state schools, rejected because they're black. Schools were telling them, "Sorry, we can't have any more in here–we've already got our one."

It was fascinating watching the profiles of some of these guys on ESPN's *SportsCentury* series. You'd hear how guys were turned away because of race, and a few minutes later you'd see reporters who covered them and historians come on and talk about "how mean these guys were." I'm sitting there thinking, "They got treated like crap their whole lives. They couldn't go to their first college of choice because the school wasn't taking any blacks or maybe taking only one, and people want to know why they are upset or bitter." They don't understand that he's got to be bitter. He ought to be bitter. How could he not be surly? He'd have to be. It's impossible not to be. "You gotta go around to the back door of the restaurant, to the kitchen, to get something to eat. You can't stay in the same hotel as your white teammates. And we're only going to have one of you per team." What do you expect—they were going to walk into the clubhouse and say, " 'Morning, good to see you guys today"?

You have ugly-ass stuff happen to you like that, what the hell you going to have, a smiley face?

I've been reading about that brother Donald Watkins from Alabama. He talked about buying the Twins, about buying the Angels. Personally, I'd love to see him involved in some other ownership ventures. Hell, he doesn't have to go to Minnesota or California either. We could use a guy of his resources right at home in Alabama. It's a complicated thing because chances are overwhelming that even if the league and owners allow him to buy in, he's never going to really be made a part of the network. He'll be an owner, but sadly he would probably never be in the mix. It is a travesty, though, that we're past the year 2000 and no person of color is the majority owner of a professional sports franchise. That's crazy.

I don't want people to think my concerns about race only deal with white people. In fact, I tend to be harder on black people who are prejudiced than white people. If you have suffered as much and as long as black people have suffered . . . If you have fought racism and seen your parents and grandparents fight racism . . . If you know the history of the suffering your own people have been through for hundreds of years and you intentionally mistreat people because of the color of their skin, that's just really, really sad to me.

And I know that point is complex, too, because resentment and bitterness are natural when you've had your ass handed to you generation after generation. You've got reason to lash out. But I look at my mother and grandmother, women who saw some really tough times and ugly bigotry, and still managed to treat people based on the way they wanted to be treated.

Not only that, but we as black folks have to do better among ourselves. We treat each other like shit. People hear me sometimes criticizing what we as black folks tend to call "the system" and say, "Man, Charles blames everything that happens to black people on 'the system.'" And "the system" is screwed up, don't get me wrong. But we still have to treat each other better. Black-on-black crime, teenage pregnancy at the rate it is, single-parent homes increasing at the rate they are . . . we ourselves have to address and solve those problems. Making your situation in society better can't happen until you start with those problems.

We live in a culture where there's so much prejudice and bias that people just start directing it anywhere, not just at people who are different but sometimes at their own people. And it's all sad and ugly. Too damn often, black people aren't even happy for accomplished black people. Guys talk about it privately among ourselves, and a lot of black people are scared to say anything publicly. But there's too much envy, which is crazy. There's enough out there for everybody to grab. Why is there envy?

When I see somebody black on television who is successful, or when I read about somebody or meet somebody who has accomplished something, I'm giddy. I see somebody black achieving something, I've got my chest all poked out.

A whole lot of times you feel that way because you know somebody and what they must have gone through to achieve something, regardless of race. But all over the world people feel good for their own people when they accomplish something. But this jealousy you see in black America sometimes, man, it's ugly and I don't understand it. I'm just trying to get to the top and send the elevator back down. Ramsey Lewis said that to me a few years ago and I thought it was profound. Getting to the top isn't the end of the process, it's the beginning. Make sure the elevator brings up somebody else.

So for some successful black people, you're caught in between two worlds you don't seem to fit in. It's a weird place for most black athletes. Even now, black people are struggling to be successful in America, to get over the hurdles or the misperceptions. A disproportionate number of the highly successful people produced by black communities probably are athletes. So when you get that type of power you have to use it. I don't think you want to hit people over the head with it, though.

The thing I want to do is pick the battles I want

to fight. I don't want to start World War III every time I'm angry about something. I was willing to fight the role model battle. I'm willing to be in there fighting the battle against racism because it's so important. But I have to pick the battles that are important to me. We as black people waste time fighting some battles that aren't worthy, or not as important as some others.

I get asked all the time about the different state flags, like the state flag of South Carolina. I think it should be taken down or changed, so as not to offend anybody. But I'm not going to waste my weekends picketing. The best thing we can do isn't picketing and it isn't spending so much time confronting the people who want to keep the flag. The best thing would be to piss them off by being successful and doing well in education and business. That's something we have a better chance of controlling. I'm more concerned with there still being only a handful of people of color who serve as the head of public relations for professional sports teams, or at the league level. There's only a sprinkling of black and Hispanic people involved in the industry of sports other than playing. And obviously, there are only a few people of color involved in ownership. I'm more concerned with owning the means of production in certain industries.

I'm not saying I don't understand why people are upset with state flags that include the Confederate flag. It's just that those people are not going to change what they feel in their hearts because they take the flag down. I understand the power of symbols, and if I had anything on my house that seriously offended someone, I'd take it down if for no other reason than common courtesy.

I guess everybody picks and chooses certain battles. One of the ones I won't back away from is the freedom to choose who you want to be with. When you marry outside of your race, as my wife and I did, you get such garbage from people of both races. People say, "Well, your kids will suffer." Sadly, that's true. Of course they only suffer because people put their prejudices off on the kids. So yeah, kids suffer because adults are hateful. But even with that, it's not like my daughter is conflicted about everything in her life every day. She doesn't wake up in the morning and wonder, "Should I study George Washington or Booker T. Washington?" That's what I tell people. It's not a daily struggle. Her life isn't one big tug-of-war. The only time kids have trouble, whether or not they are the products of interracial marriages, is when people put ignorant shit in their heads.

People should be able to go out and date whoever they want to and it's nobody's damn business. And that's that. I think anybody who disagrees with that basic freedom to associate with, befriend and date whoever you want to is full of shit and has some kind of agenda they need to seriously think about.

Life in the Public Eye

I've had plenty of people tell me it appears I enjoy being famous. But I've always disagreed with that. It's that I enjoy meeting people. There are only two ways to go about life if you are famous: enjoy this damn life or be miserable. People say, "Do you enjoy being a celebrity?" And I say, "Not really." When I was playing I wish I could have played basketball and made a lot of money, period.

When you're in public life, no matter who you are, you're either going to learn how to enjoy it, especially meeting people, or be a miserable jerk. A lot of famous people go through their whole lives not wanting to be bothered, with bodyguards hanging around all the time, or staying to themselves. I've always thought that wasn't going to be me. It didn't seem to be an enjoyable way to go about it. Like Jack Nicholson says, this is as good as it gets. So if you're successful at something and you become famous for it, that's as good as it gets. So why walk around moping all the time? That trips me out. And especially if you're healthy physically and financially and your family and friends are healthy, what the hell is there to mope around and complain about or have all these people trying to shield you from folks?

I don't enjoy the limelight as much as people might think. You think I want to talk to the press every day or accommodate everybody's wishes all the time? Hell no. But I'm the luckiest damn guy in the world, and I'm not going to walk around being miserable. I'm going to have fun with this. I just believe in accommodating people whenever possible. It wears you out, having to do it all the time, especially when you're tired or you have serious things on your mind. But I just believe that signing autographs or posing for pictures with people or sitting and talking with people who want to meet you is all part of what goes with being a public person. I don't turn people down for autographs unless I'm eating or I'm trying to keep on schedule or there are so many that there's just no way to sign them all.

It's an honor to play professional sports for a living. It's an honor to entertain people or make them feel better or whatever it is they feel when they're watching you. And it's an honor to be a celebrity. And I just refuse to stop living my life and enjoying great restaurants or hanging out with friends because I'm a public person.

It's not as easy as it sounds, because I've been arrested I think five or six times for getting into altercations with people in public. But each and every time I've been acquitted. I just wish when reporters write or talk about this they would get the whole story and tell it accurately. I have never bothered anybody in public or anywhere else. I've never walked up to anybody and initiated anything. Famous people don't go out to bother people; they go out to do the same things everybody else does. But there's always some drunk with liquid courage who wants to get some attention or make you notice him or make an ass of himself with the people in your group.

You know what I'm thinking when I see one of these guys? "Hey man, it's not my fault your damn life sucks, or is so ordinary you're looking to spice it up by starting trouble with people minding their own business just because you've seen them on TV or read about 'em in the newspaper or a magazine. I'm sorry you don't like your life, but let me enjoy mine."

The funniest thing of all is after you've both been arrested and they have to come to court, they've got this look on their faces like, "Oh my God! All of this!" I've had a couple of them come to me afterward and say, "You know, I've had to do twenty-five interviews. All these reporters were standing outside the courthouse with notebooks and microphones! Man, I'm sorry. I was drunk that night. I didn't realize what your life was like and how public everything about your life is." And I've said, "No shit, asshole. The next time you go out and see a famous person or some public figure, leave him alone, don't harass him. Cut out the BS." Because they have no idea, they don't understand the stories that are going to be in the press, that reporters will be calling them, how it's going to look when their lives are exposed to public scrutiny.

I've lived my life in the public eye for twenty years, and I know that if I get arrested or something negative happens that it's a really incredibly big deal. I know on *Headline News* you'll see a picture of Barkley every eighteen and forty-eight minutes after the hour. And I'll be the cover story of *USA Today*. But some fool who's never dealt with all this, who wants to punch you because he's drunk and he wants to brag to his boys the next day . . . when he sobers up he's like, "You have to deal with this every day of your life?" I say, "Man, it's not what you thought it was, is it?" It was a big news story when David Stern told me he wanted me to have a bodyguard, and I understood his concern. But I think it's easier for a famous person to go relatively incognito, or if not incognito then to just get around more easily if you're by yourself, with no entourage. I don't want to think about calling my bodyguard before I go out to do something. I want to put my clothes on, go out and do whatever. I don't believe in getting the entourage together before you can go out and live your life. I think what happens is the extra attention you draw by having somebody guarding you pisses people off more. And when they're drunk you're like a magnet and they're thinking, "Look at this guy, he thinks he's a big deal because he's got his entourage with him." If I'm by myself there's less of a commotion.

The funny thing is, I'm not some asshole who

goes around beating up people. Anybody who has spent any time with me knows I meet a million people, and I've had a problem that became a serious problem with five or six crazy people.

A long time ago, I adopted what I call the 50-50 rule: no matter what you do in your life, 50 percent of the people are going to like it and 50 percent will dislike it. . . . If you're out there and you miss a putt or miss a free throw with the game on the line, half the people are going to sympathize with you and the other half are going to say, "That sorry bastard choked like a dog!" In Philly, after a game I'd have 500 people standing and waiting for me. I've got dinner reservations and family members or guests waiting for me. If I sign 250 autographs, 250 hate my ass. You can sit there for an hour, hungry and ready to go to dinner and being rude to your family or friends, and you can't please everybody.

Seriously, I get a thousand requests a week. And I try to do three to five things every week, and some of them take hours. But the people you can't accommodate, a lot of them get really angry, which reminds me that no matter how much you do, a lot of people are going to be upset. Even if you signed a thousand autographs every day you couldn't please everybody.

That's why I say, "I'm going to do my own thing, say what I want to say, take stands I feel like taking even if they're unpopular."

E-mail, telephone and alcohol are the three primary ways people get brave. People come up to you after a couple of drinks and want to tell you what to say. And I tell them, "It's okay to tell me you disagree with me, but don't ever tell me what I can say and not say."

But even with that being a downside, I enjoy the vast majority of the people I meet. I've had so many rewarding experiences, some of them from chance meetings, some from people just coming up and introducing themselves and wanting to talk about common experiences or something. I'm not going to let a tiny percentage of people stop me from enjoying that. I knew pretty early on that I was going to be in control as much as possible. I always say that I played basketball, it didn't play me. But fame plays you. You're only famous because somebody's making money off you. You can't control what anybody else does. You've got to make sure you make and keep your money, and otherwise try to live your life to the fullest extent that you want to. Some people aren't that extroverted, but I am. I want to enjoy myself, as well as the people I come into contact with. It's such a great life, why wouldn't I?

That's one of the things that I find funny when people say my life isn't complete because I didn't win an NBA championship. I have to laugh because with the exceptions of maybe Tiger Woods and Michael Jordan, I don't think I'd trade places with anybody. And I don't even think I'd trade places with them, because the attention and inconvenience they have to put up with are several times more than mine.

Anyway, what else in life could I need when my life is pretty unbelievable already?

Being Rich

I've probably lost between $600,000 and $700,000 lending money to my friends and relatives. Most of the friends I've loaned money to won't even speak to me now. It's the strangest damned thing. It's weird being rich and black because you're caught between two worlds. Being rich really puts you in a predominantly white world. Overwhelmingly, everybody you work with outside of sports is white. But you don't just stop liking things about the life you've lived, your old friends and your boys. You've outgrown most of them, really, but you really want to maintain relationships. And they want to borrow money and you do it. You say yes and it's almost like buying friendship to stay in good with 'em. And then they turn on you, too. If you say no, it's like, "You're not going to give me any more money?"

And the line they use on you is, "Oh, you ain't the same guy anymore!" They tell you how you've gone big-time and how they know you don't want to be around them anymore. Next thing you know you've lent them hundreds and hundreds of thousands of dollars, and I'm not exaggerating. I've got the receipts to prove it. But you know what? I'm not going to ever ask their asses for my money. And the money, on some level, is irrelevant because I can do without the money. But it bothers me more that I've lost those friendships. You're just caught, not really certain what to do.

Guys in similar situations joke about it, how you've got to watch your family, too. Man, your family goes through money like crazy. We all know guys in the NBA, great guys, who have a lot of brothers and sisters and they're all driving Mercedeses. Hey, you can get your brother a Hyundai. Everybody in the house doesn't have to have a Mercedes-Benz.

I built my mother and grandmother houses, and my brothers houses, and I've bought them two or three cars at least. I had to get to a point where I said, "No, hey, that's enough." As much as I love my family, I have to say, "We've got to stop this." You hear some real horror stories from your teammates. I'm fortunate because I played a long time and made great money. But the average career is four, five years. And those guys aren't necessarily making a ton of money. But guys don't think to themselves, "Hey, I might only be in the league two or three years and I better really watch what I'm doing." No, guys think, "Well, I'm making several million dollars a year; I won't ever be able to spend it all." But after you take out taxes, even on $10 million a year, and support all your freeloaders, you're like, "I'd better get on the right track with this." I tell them, "When it's over, make sure you've got something."

I've got guys right now who had a deal with Nike, and now call me to get them shoes from Nike. When you're out, you're out. We call them "owls" because when they call after they retire the person at the other end of the phone says, "Who?" When the party is over, there are no more shoes, no more free tickets. Ex-NBA players don't get free tickets to games. You need to have saved and invested. I was very fortunate when I was a young player to have veteran guys pull me aside and counsel me on what to do. My first agent cheated me out of a lot of money. Luckily, Julius Erving and Moses Malone taught me so much about a lot of things, including money.

I don't know if it's a black thing or not . . . maybe it's just because most of the guys in the NBA are black and that was my environment. But when I first got to the pros, I bought something like six cars. And Doc and Moses made me sell 'em. They told me, "Look, man, you can only drive one car. What the hell are you doing with six? If you drive one car, sell the other five and invest that money wisely and just let the damn money grow, that will become enough money to buy twenty cars in five to ten years." Something else they told me that was very important, and I'm glad they didn't just sit back and tell me what I wanted to hear. They told me, "You don't have to drive a lot of flashy, expensive cars, spend a lot of money on jewelry to get attention. Stop trying to impress people; everybody already knows who the hell you are." And it was really profound. They were right, of course. You don't need to drive a Bentley; you'd be better served with the money being wisely invested. I've got my expensive hobbies. I like to go to Las Vegas and gamble, which everybody knows, and I love golf. But I

have two cars now, SUVs, and I don't have any entourages.

The first time it hit me that my life was probably
going to change–I mean be really different and that I
wasn't going to have to be poor–was the day I left
home for college. I had only left Alabama a couple of
times before my first road trip playing college basketball. My mom and I went to visit some in-laws in
Youngstown, Ohio, one summer. But hell, that was a
bad neighborhood also. And I went to Compton, California, one summer before I went to high school. I
went to visit my dad one summer and almost got
killed in some gang thing.

I don't know if there were Crips and Bloods then,
I don't know what or who it was. We got into a
fight with some guys and ended up running, and I've
never been that scared in my life. I never went back
either. That was my first experience in California.
Some guys I was with, we just wound up wandering
through some bad neighborhood and met up with
some guys . . . and we couldn't do anything about it.
The police couldn't or wouldn't do anything about
it either. But that's what happens in all-black neighborhoods. It wouldn't happen in Buckhead in Atlanta,
I'll tell you that.

I went to Buckhead a couple of weeks after the Ray Lewis incident happened. I got there on a Sunday night, and Buckhead was closed down. They closed the clubs for a while, the restaurants, everything. I asked a guy what was going on and he said Buckhead was shut down, completely locked down for a while on Sunday nights. They weren't going to let people tear up Buckhead. That's the power and influence that result from having wealth.

Sometimes you need a reality check, just to be reconnected to everyday life. You need to be reminded of just how much money you have, and the issues you used to have to consider before you had any money. Sometimes friends will say, "Hey, man, I'm coming to visit you in two months." And I'll say, "Why the hell are you telling me that now?" And they'll say, "Because I had to buy my airline tickets today, asshole, so it won't cost a million dollars." See, I have no perception of that now, because I never flew on a plane when I was on welfare, and now I've been rich for a long time and haven't had to consider that. And since September 11, I've pretty much been flying in private planes. So it's definitely a reality check when somebody calls me saying, "I need to keep this airfare under $200." And I'm like, "Damn, you need to buy a ticket two months in advance to fly on this ratty airline? In coach?" See, I have no perception of that.

I'll tell you another reality check: Enron and WorldCom. Half the executives at Enron have participated in congressional hearings, but nobody's in jail yet. They've stolen millions of dollars and hid it real good. And all those working people, some of them just working-class poor people, have lost their jobs, their pensions, their 401(k) plans, and they're waiting there, like, "What's next?"

Nothing's next, that's what's next.

They stole poor people's money. Rich people can steal shit and get away with it, that's how the game works. How many people at fault for what happened at Enron and WorldCom are going to jail? And whoever does go to jail is going to one of those little fluff prisons for five years, and when he gets out he's getting most of his money anyway. Who's worse off, the guy who spent every damn cent he's got to put his kids through school and doesn't have his pension anymore or some rich thief who's coming out of a fluff prison to pick up a couple of million?

I'm a little sensitive about this whole thing because I've got so many friends from my playing days in Houston who worked for Enron. They're all walking around like zombies, saying, "Hey, man, I lost my job, I lost my pension." I know between fifteen and twenty people who worked at Enron, good friends in Houston. Lost their life's savings. What recourse do they have?

So even though I need a reality check every once in a while, I never lose sight of the fact that we make a lot of money. The average salary in the NBA now is approximately $3 million per year. Guys who can't play a lick can make that. But it's short-lived, and people are making a lot more money off of us than we're making. Guys think they're controlling the process, when all they're getting is royalties. I know how much money I've made, and I know I was getting, like, 2 percent of shoe sales. And I'm thinking, "Damn, if I'm only getting 2 percent, and never more than 5 percent on anything, and I'm getting a $700,000 royalty check from the sale of shoes that cost $125 a pair, then a lot of people are making money on me."

And that's nothing compared to what people have made off Michael Jordan and Tiger Woods. Everybody has made money on them. Look at the boost television has gotten from Tiger Woods. The television executives must lose their minds if Tiger isn't on the leader board on Sunday, because he's the money generator. I know they made a ton of money on me because I see my jerseys and shoes everywhere.

The guys producing this stuff, the guys who own these companies and teams, are way too smart to be losing money. And we ain't getting the first cut. They're all megamillionaires. Remember what Jerry Krause said when he broke up the Chicago Bulls. He said, "It ain't the players, it's the organization." The organization ran the greatest player ever out of Chicago. The club is still doing well financially. The team is appreciating. They've got a new arena. That's the perfect example of sports being a business more than anything else. Everybody who plays professionally ought to stop and think, "If they did that to Michael Jordan they'll sure as hell do it to me." Was I shocked? No. I remember when Michael got his first $30 million contract, in 1996. We were in Lake Tahoe. And he said, "Can you believe Jerry Reinsdorf told me, 'There's no man that's worth this much money'?" This is the guy who made Jerry Reinsdorf, the Bulls chairman, a billionaire, made it so that the franchise is playing in a shiny new arena, gave an identity to a team that didn't exist on any national level before Michael got there, and damn sure hadn't won anything. He played at Kmart prices, relatively speaking, before that. It's the best example ever of sports being a business first and foremost. It's the best example of what revenues are generated, what owners take away and what players take away.

As long as the Bulls were getting Michael for below-market value, everything was cool. But then when they had to start paying him, no. So when Scottie's contract was up, it's like, "Nope, we're not paying both of y'all." The biggest thing of all in this is merchandising. It's a billion-dollar-plus business. Tell me they weren't making money. If Michael could have gotten one dollar for every No. 23 jersey I've seen with my own eyes in my travels, he'd have more money than most Third World countries.

The funny thing about this is that Michael is so damn cheap. Michael ain't the most popular guy in Las Vegas. He'll win $1 million in the casino and not tip the people. I don't like to just walk by homeless people. If I see a homeless person, I want to give them some money, even if it's just a little something. Michael saw me giving a homeless person some money one day and grabbed me and said, "Quit doing that. If they're able to ask you for some spare change they can say, 'Welcome to McDonald's, can I help you please?' "

As important as money is in the business of professional sports, there's real irony in that you can't
allow it to be in the equation when you walk into
the gym for practice or for games or for a meeting
or workouts. You just can't. Athletes are just like
anybody else. We've always cared about money. We
care about setting ourselves up for life and being
able to take care of our families and friends, and we
want to afford nice things and a great lifestyle. But we
did not talk seriously about contracts in the locker
room for most of my career. Lately, that's started to
change. You've got guys now talking about whether
they're going to get the max, or whether they're going to opt out of their contracts. We never discussed
that stuff during the season, and it never mattered
when we got in a room as a team. If a guy even
thought he was going to discuss that stuff, we'd say,
"Hey, let's go and play, and all that stuff will be
worked out when the season's over, 'cause you can't
change it today. If you can play, if you go out there
and perform and we play and have a good season,
you'll always get your money in the end." All this "I'm
a free agent, let me see what I can get on the open
market" stuff, or "I can get the max if they'll let my
agent work out a sign-and-trade." When you've got

your best players talking about that stuff, you've got a problem.

And Michael probably deserves more credit for keeping that stuff out of the mix than anybody, because he was a guy who was clearly underpaid for the first ten years of his career, but never bitched or talked about any of it. And guys had to fall in line behind him on that issue. How are they going to bring that up in a locker room if Michael didn't? If the best player in the league handles that privately, and sends a signal publicly that he's going to give them–the fans–their money's worth first and foremost, then guys around the league have to pretty much follow his lead. I think that's an important part of greatness, believing that if you make yourself the best you can be, you will be compensated. And not the other way around.

Johnny Miller said something real crazy during an NBC golf telecast one day. He said that Tiger's under no pressure out there because he already had his financial life set, everything in place. I think it's the total opposite. Look at all these young boys now, in every sport, individual and team sports, who play a few years and get out. They get all the money early and they lose their obsession and after a few years they just don't have it in 'em to go out there and work as hard as they did earlier. Money isn't what Tiger's playing for. Hell yeah, he wants it and deserves it. But it can't be what he's playing for. His motivation runs so much deeper than that. The pressure on Tiger, like the pressure on Michael, is to be the greatest ever every time he steps to the tee or stands over a putt.

Scams and Double Standards

The punishment for priests who confess to having had sex with minors, and for priests proven to have had sex with minors is really simple:

They ought to be put in jail.

I want to make sure I'm clear on my position on what should happen to grown men who have sex with children. They should be convicted and thrown in jail.

Thrown.

In.

Jail.

What we seem to do best now is hold hearings or

convene meetings. We don't need meetings to figure this out. The Catholic Church shouldn't spend another minute or another dollar gathering bishops together in Rome or flying cardinals in from all over the world. If you're having sex with little kids, you need to be taken not only out of the church, but off the streets. We, as a society, can't spend one minute hiding behind political correctness on this one. If your ass is caught having sex with a minor, you're a pedophile and you've got to serve jail time.

I guess if R. Kelly had become a priest he'd be fine because then he'd be protected from the laws that any other pedophile is subject to.

We don't need to adopt any more policies. We don't need to have any more conferences. The Catholic Church needs to stand for children and decency and the U.S. government ought to start prosecuting people and putting their asses in jail. The people who knew about children being sexually abused by priests and protected them ought to be prosecuted as accomplices and be subject to jail time. Law enforcement officials shouldn't even be leaving punishment up to the church. When did the United States start letting criminal acts against little kids go unprosecuted? The same church that opposes gay marriages and abortion rights has priests who sexually abuse children and does nothing but hold conferences?

I'm sorry, this is a zero-tolerance situation. How can you claim the moral authority any church needs if the people who are supposed to be leading the church are violating little kids? This is sick, and yes it is serious enough to make people pay for their actions. I believe in forgiveness and tolerance, but I also believe in punishment. This doesn't really have anything to do with Catholicism. Yeah, in this case it involves the Catholic Church. But I don't care who it is. If violating our children doesn't call for punishment, what the hell does? If we're not going to get angry and put a stop to this, then when are we going to?

If I see something that isn't right, I've got to hit it. This is why I can't wait to do the CNN show this fall. We're going to call it like we see it and we're not ducking any issues and we're not sugarcoating anything, especially the serious stuff.

Probably nothing is as serious as children being abused, but there's other stuff that needs addressing. First it was Enron and then it was WorldCom involved in all this financial fraud. I was watching television one night this summer when the WorldCom scandal first broke, and there was a woman with tears in her eyes asking, "When are these people going to jail?" And I'm talking to the TV, saying, "Lady, rich folks don't go to jail; poor folks go to jail."

If some penny-ante drug dealer gets caught making a $10,000 drug deal, he's going to jail and his house and car are going to be confiscated, which is what ought to happen. But Martha Stewart ain't going to jail. She'll sell all of her stock the day before the company announces huge losses. We can't possibly think Enron and WorldCom are the only ones guilty of this stuff, can we?

I'm sitting there riding the stationary bike and watching these lying, stealing executives on TV. The top executives refuse to testify before Congress about a $4 billion accounting scandal. The financial markets are in turmoil. The employees are losing their jobs and their pensions and their 401(k)s, and these guys—top guys, mind you—are refusing to talk to Congress. Come on now. Constitutional right to not talk? What about working people's rights not to be ripped off and defrauded?

How many billions did WorldCom underreport or improperly account for? Four billion, right? How do you simply misplace $4 billion? Four billion doesn't just disappear. Look, $50,000 is a mistake. But four billion? Four billion is stealing. Those are damn crooks. A guy buys a $15 million house in Florida with money that ain't his and he's not in jail? That guy's got to go to jail except . . . we all know he ain't going to jail. What's the worst that's going to happen to his ass? He's going to resign. Resign! Why the hell would he need to work if he's already paid for a $15 million house? And by the way, where was the SEC during all this? Why shouldn't we think that the people who are supposed to be holding people accountable are in cahoots with the crooks? The only thing that's going to come out of this, and out of Enron, is that some poor people are going to be poorer 'cause they've been robbed of the little money they had in their pensions and retirement funds and the crooks are going to walk away with a slap on the wrist, if that.

Poor people and working people just have no voice at all. They get bombarded by people trying to take what little they have. I want to do a show on what a rip-off credit cards are. Credit Cards enable somebody who barely makes ends meet to buy a $300 item and over time pay $900 for it because of 19 percent interest rates. And the ones who have bad credit pay a higher rate than that. Tell me this isn't a rip-off. Make the guy who can least afford it pay more. I use two credit cards, both of them American Express, where you have to pay off the balance every month. The biggest obstacle for poor people, besides having no money, is giving in to instant gratification and deferred payment. You're trying to make ends meet, so you keep paying the minimum to have some money left over, except the interest and the growing balance are kicking your ass.

I don't want to hear anybody say, "Charles, why do you care since you're not poor?" I used to be poor. I've been rich less than half my life. There are just so many scams out there and this is one of them. I guess scams and double standards are things that I'm very disturbed by. I'll tell you another double standard, and this is a very sensitive issue to deal with but it needs addressing. People just sit in judgment and decide who gets a pass and who gets hammered.

Darryl Kile, the Cardinals pitcher who died of heart-related issues this summer in his hotel room at thirty-three years old, was a really good guy by all accounts. I mean, anybody who knew him said he was a really good guy. And it's tragic when a man with a wife and young children passes away in the prime of his life. It's just sad whether the guy is a professional athlete or a plumber.

What I'm wondering about, though, is why it was so glossed over that marijuana was found in Kile's room when he died. I mean, it was reported, and pretty much just dismissed. It was reported that the marijuana had nothing to do with his death, and there's no reason to think it did. But man, if that happened to a guy people didn't like, it would have been a week's worth of news. If someone judged to be a "bad guy" had died with marijuana in his room, the hammer would have come down on his ass.

Why is it that Patrick Roy gets arrested for spousal abuse and very little is said about it, but Jason Kidd is involved in the same situation and is just hammered? I mean, I don't know Patrick Roy and it shouldn't be important whether I know him. Yes, Patrick Roy's case involved property and ultimately it was dismissed, but it's not like nothing happened. So who makes up these rules on who's a good guy and who's a bad guy? And is that how we want to decide how people are treated publicly? Who decides who gets a pass on this stuff? I just think we've got to be really careful about double standards and how they're applied. Wrong is wrong, and if we're going to hold people accountable for actions, then let's be evenhanded about the punishment–even if the person in question is a priest.

The Worst Thing About Playing Professional Sports

The only time professional athletes are ever completely healthy all year, and by that I mean feeling their 100 percent best, is the first day of training camp. After that, it's sprains and muscle pulls and tissue damage and bruises and dislocations the rest of the season. After the first few years of my career, I was taking injections once every couple of weeks and/or pills every few days. And I wasn't the only one taking anti-inflammatory agents. Although there's no proof of what exactly led to Alonzo Mourning's kidney problems, there's a whole lot of fear in the basketball community–particularly among players–that anti-inflammatories had something to do with it, that taking them in order to play took a toll on a vital organ. And if that turns out to be true, there are going to be a lot of terrified professional athletes out there, and a whole lot of people needing organ donations because we've all done it.

People who haven't played professional sports cannot understand the physical demands pro athletes are under, and the amount of discomfort, aches and pains guys endure just to put on the uniform and play. I would never try to diminish guys who played at the semipro level or the college level. But a college basketball player, for example, plays thirty games a year, while a guy in the NBA plays a hundred if his team goes deep into the playoffs. There's nothing like the physical demands on a pro athlete. Unless you've run into Karl Malone's body or been slammed by Bill Laimbeer, you just can't have any idea. When I would drive to the basket against the Detroit Pistons in the 1980s when they had the "Bad Boys" I would say to myself, "Just close your eyes and let the ball go because you're gonna get hammered. Just go up strong and finish because they're gonna knock the hell out of you." And they did. Most people, even people who are fairly tough and athletic, couldn't withstand one game of that, much less ten to twelve years of it night after night.

My first season in the NBA, 1984–85, I only played 14, 15 minutes a game and I remember thinking, "Oh, this ain't so bad physically." But after my second year, when I started playing more than 30 minutes a game, it changed. When you start playing killer minutes you notice. You feel the toll that all those minutes, all that jumping and running and banging, are taking on your body. I remember my sense of it changing to "Man, this is damaging my body." You hit the wall as a rookie, but that's fatigue from never having had to play so many minutes and so many games in college. But pain is different. It's much worse. You dislocate a finger two or three times a season, and after a while your fingers aren't pointing in the same direction. Six times I've been operated on. Both knees have been 'scoped multiple times. I had to have my torn triceps repaired, then my quad at the end of my career. You feel an obligation to play anyway, especially the stars in any sport, because you know how much your teammates are depending on you, you know how much the fans are hoping to see you play; that's why they pay all that money for those tickets. You want to be out there because you want your team to win and you know how difficult that is if you're the best player, or one of the two best players, and you're unable to play. But the overlooked thing is how management rushes athletes back to play. They're notorious for it.

Anytime an athlete gets injured, you hear or read the next day that he'll be out two to three weeks or four to six weeks, or some specific period of time. That's based on what the team physician and trainers tell him. So they tell you that you'll be out four to six weeks–everybody knows because it's in the newspaper and on TV–but after you miss one week they start asking you, "How long are you going to be out?" And you're thinking, "You just told every reporter in the world I'm going to be out four to six weeks, so why are you asking me after one week how long I'm going to be out?"

The last time I got 'scoped–I was playing in Houston–I played in a regular season game exactly two weeks later. I had sprained a knee, got 'scoped on a Sunday, and played on a Sunday fourteen days later. There's no question I came back too fast. There's pressure coming from everywhere to play as quickly as you can, even though nobody really knows the extent of some of these injuries and nobody knows or cares about the long-term damage you're doing to yourself.

That's the culture of the sport, and it's something we accept. When a guy is hurt and he keeps playing, you're thinking, "Aw, man, look at that guy still out there playing–I've got to keep playing if he's playing." So you stay in the lineup anyway. Or you might miss one game and come back sooner than you should. Several times I've asked physicians outside team sports how long I would be inactive if I wasn't a professional athlete. In other words, how long would a normal person take to come back from this injury I'm expected to recover from in four to six weeks? And they've told me, well, probably six weeks instead of four, or eight to ten instead of six. You hear stories from your first day in any professional sports league. We all know stories about guys in the NFL playing with fractured legs and broken bones and fingers nearly severed.

I hope people were really listening to the details that were reported about the day Korey Stringer of the Minnesota Vikings died from heat exhaustion in training camp. He came out of practice twice, and he was vomiting. And the guy sitting at home listening to this is figuring, "Well, if he was vomiting and came out twice, he must have known there was something seriously wrong." People who haven't been there have no idea how many times guys vomit during an NFL training camp or have to come out for a few plays, then go right back in because of the pressure to keep playing. Now, that's the most extreme case because it's a tragic example, that a young man with a family died because he felt he just had to play through some kind of suffering. But the pressure to keep playing is tremendous. People have no idea.

And there really is a difference between being injured and being hurt in the culture of professional sports. And you have to figure it out yourself. You're hurt all the time, and by that I mean having sore ankles and back spasms that wouldn't let some people sleep at night. Athletes don't get nearly enough credit for playing with pain season after season. But being injured is another story altogether. And one of the saddest things in sports is when a guy is injured—not just hurt but injured—and he's made to feel like some kind of slacker and the public and the media are on his ass even though he shouldn't even be trying to play.

Early in my career in Philadelphia, the 76ers owner Harold Katz questioned whether Andrew Toney's feet were really injured. Andrew had missed some time and was really struggling with his feet, and everybody was expressing an opinion as to why he was missing games. And Philadelphia is not the kind of place where you can just shrug off that kind of criticism and ridicule. I need to point out that this was happening in the mid-1980s, before MRI tests were around, or at least before they were commonly used. Team physicians had to read X-rays, and stress fractures apparently didn't show up on X-rays. But because he was made to feel like he had to play, Andrew tried to play. And he shouldn't have been playing at all, not at all, not even a little bit. A couple of years later, as new medical technology was put to use, the doctors found Andrew had all kinds of stress fractures in his feet. The guy was injured. I felt guilty for thinking at times that he wasn't injured as seriously as he really was. I think about it now because Andrew Toney was probably the best player in his prime that I played with. Doc and Moses had already had their best years by then, but Andrew was just coming into his prime when I got to Philly in the fall of 1984.

My very first practice, there's Toney shooting jumpers, and he's in the process of making something like fifty straight shots. I called my friends after practice and said, "This guy, Andrew Toney, may be the best shooter I've ever seen." It was unbelievable the way he shot. Man, we could have done some damage together. He was just a tough old southern dude. (He's also the one who got me started playing golf.) And he wasn't the kind of guy who would ever complain, so it was hard to know exactly when he was in pain or how much pain he was in.

But one night, I'm sitting on the bench next to him. And you know how close guys are sitting next to each other on a bench. I was moving around and accidentally kicked his feet and tears literally came to his eyes. I saw that and I thought, "My God, there must be something seriously wrong with this man's feet."

I never had anything quite like that. But I know the cumulative effect is going to be serious. I hurt my back the first time when I was playing in Philly. And I would have back problems the rest of my career. I know my body's going to be shot when I get older. A lot of my friends are pro athletes and their bodies are going to be shot, too. I go to these charity events and all the legends are limping around so badly. Right now, when I play golf with John Elway and Dan Marino, we've got the same ex-athlete walk and we're just forty years old. The way we're moving now, I look at the legends and I know that's going to be me in a few years. That's the biggest negative about playing professional sports. People ask me about being approached in public and signing autographs and being asked to do so many things. And while that might inconvenience you and consume your time, it doesn't take a toll on your health. But you make your peace with it by simply saying, "This is the price you have to pay to play." Your last two, three or four years, it's hard just getting out of bed in the morning. Past thirty-two, thirty-three, thirty-four years old, it's a struggle and I don't care who you are. Hakeem Olajuwon, Patrick Ewing, John Stockton . . . I don't like to see them struggling. People say it's amazing that John and Karl can still play like that at forty, and that's true. But these guys coming into the league now couldn't hold their jockstraps when they were thirty. Most of my career, I played above the basket whenever I needed to, or wanted to. But late in my career, I would see guys flying to the basket and think, "Damn, these guys are running fast and jumping high."

That's why the notion of coming back to play sounds great, but it doesn't feel great. You love the game so much you want to play, but your body isn't cooperating with your spirit. I told Michael Jordan, when we were talking about my coming back, that he might have been getting in shape but I was just getting tired. And as amazing an athlete as Michael is, his knees just wouldn't cooperate with him when he came back to play with the Wizards. The shocking thing is that he hadn't needed more 'scopes before on his knee, considering the jumping and running he did for thirteen years. Every basketball, football, hockey and baseball player in the world could probably have at least one knee cleaned out right now with a 'scope. But that doesn't cure the tendinitis or the arthritis or restore the cartilage.

And I don't know how football players can ever have their health. The collisions those guys have are violent and damaging enough. And then on top of that, they've got to play on AstroTurf, which is the worst invention in the history of professional football. I see ex-NFL players now, guys in their fifties and sixties, and I just say to myself, "Damn."

Tiger and the Masters

In the March 11 edition of *Sports Illustrated,* the cover of which was graced with a picture of me without a shirt breaking out of chains—it was carefully thought out, planned and meant to be symbolic—I said some things about Tiger Woods, Augusta National and the Masters that pissed off a lot of people. Specifically, I said, "Look what they're doing at Augusta. They're lengthening the course for one reason: to hurt Tiger." I don't believe that the course was lengthened specifically to stop Tiger from winning, but I do believe that his winning all the time must make people who run the Masters tournament uncomfortable.

It's not Tiger's personality–not yet anyway–to speak out about stuff that might be controversial to some people. It's not like him to talk about whether this thing was designed to specifically stop him and whether that involves race. But I'm not worried about saying the proper thing. I think it needs to be examined. And I don't think I'm the only one who feels like this was aimed more at Tiger than at anybody else. And even if I am the only one who felt that way, then I'll say it anyway. People want me to give the benefit of the doubt to Augusta National and the people who run the Masters tournament. Why? Benefit of the doubt is something you earn through past actions. We know what the past actions have been at Augusta National: to exclude black golfers, to make black and Hispanic golfers feel unwelcome, as if they better not even think of the idea of showing up to play there. There are a few members of color now, but that's happened in the last few years. It ain't exactly the U.N. up in that clubhouse.

So you mean to tell me that all of a sudden, after all these years of discrimination, the people who run Augusta just became color-blind? We're supposed to believe that their decisions regarding a golfer of color, the one who was kicking their course in the ass, were made without any consideration of his race? Why would we believe that? You can believe that BS if you want but don't ask me to. Maybe I would believe it if the history of Augusta was different. But Augusta National is what it is, a great golf course and a symbol of prejudice and racism in the South. It's a symbol of what people who run traditional southern institutions think of black people.

The people who take me on about my views on Augusta National . . . I'd like to ask them one thing: Does Tiger's winning change everything that ever happened at Augusta National? Does it affect the lives of the black people who've been denied access? Does it change the fact that most of the black people on the grounds can still only caddie there? I love Tiger like a brother and I'm glad he's got three Green Jackets. But is Augusta National a completely different institution now because of it? Is the history of Augusta any different now? I don't know this for sure, but I'm thinking that Tiger winning at Augusta allows a whole lot of people an easy way to feel better about ugly things like exclusion. Tiger wins, so they get an easy way out of dealing with some real ugly stuff, some of their own bigoted feelings they've been carrying around but don't want to deal with.

This issue is certainly not limited to Augusta National, or even to race. I am personally uncomfortable playing golf anywhere that doesn't admit minorities or women as members.

People have to deal with this stuff even though it's difficult, and not just try to sweep it under the rug. And it doesn't get resolved in a hurry. Prejudice and racism scar people for life. But we as a society never really discuss that stuff at length because it isn't comfortable. The black goaltender who plays for the Carolina Hurricanes, the backup goaltender, is a guy named Kevin Weekes. He played great for Carolina early in the playoffs coming off the bench, and he helped the Hurricanes get to the Stanley Cup finals. That sorry-ass franchise never had been close to the finals before. And even though this guy was mostly the backup (to Arturs Irbe), the team couldn't have gotten to the finals without Weekes coming in to play the way he did several different times during the playoffs. Anyway, somebody threw a banana at him and hit him in the head during the playoffs. Yes, it was reported, but it was touched on just for a minute on *SportsCenter.* I'm sure—or at least I hope—it got some major attention down around Raleigh because it was local or regional news in North Carolina. But nationally, there was hardly anything on it. Wasn't that worth a longer discussion, that a black goalie gets hit in the head by a banana in 2002? You know the symbolism is, "Here's this black guy in a predominately white sport and he's being called a monkey." Don't get me wrong now, I'm glad ESPN reported it, but don't tell me that in 2002 a black man playing goalie for a professional hockey team and gets hit by some bigot throwing a banana isn't worth more than just a mention. You don't just give five seconds to a story like that and go straight to a damn baseball score. That shit deserves some examination and some comment, doesn't it?

I'm thinking, "Man, there's some shit still going on out here in the world," but people aren't saying anything about it. Do they not think about it, or just not say anything about it? Bad stuff just happens and it goes unreported or there's barely a mention of it before we go back to business as usual. The Weekes story reminded me of the Bobby Jones story going into the Masters. ESPN did a *SportsCentury* profile on Bobby Jones, and I know magazine articles and entire books have been written on the life of Bobby Jones because he's a historic figure in golf. You can't write the history of golf without telling the story of Bobby

Jones. The *SportsCentury* piece was talking about him being the greatest golfer ever . . . then just like that you hear, "Oh, and he wouldn't have anything to do with black people." Okay, I'm exaggerating a little bit, but after a couple of more comments by people saying the same thing, that was pretty much the extent of the treatment of Bobby Jones as a racist? Most times when you see or read stories on Bobby Jones there isn't even that much on what a bigot he was. Usually, it's like somebody shrugs and says, "Well, it's not that big a deal because he was a product of his time." What kind of shit is that when things just get explained away by the phrase "product of his time"? Is that supposed to convince us that it was cool, because a lot of other white people did it, too?

A lot of stuff that happened in the South and stuff that still happens today makes me angry as hell. But those times in the South were more complex than that. Some people didn't just go along. Weren't there a bunch of courageous white people who got their asses bit by police dogs and sprayed with water hoses and beat with police batons trying to fight racism? They were right there in the front of marches alongside black people all across the South. They were right there at those lunch counters protesting segregation in public places. They were on the front lines hand in hand with black people. They were white and southern, so what the hell were they a product of?

Tell you something else: no black athlete or performer could be portrayed in mainstream media as a hero if he openly hated white people. He was a product of his time? No damn way. That excuse would never fly for a black athlete or entertainer. And after I said something about it, after I commented about it on TBS or TNT, people came up to me and said, "How could you call Bobby Jones a racist? You shouldn't say that." Hey, ESPN just told me about Bobby Jones in the *SportsCentury* profile, and from all indications he was a bigot. I didn't know Bobby Jones personally. He'd be 129 years old by now. I can only go by ESPN's reporting. And it's not like anybody has come forward to dispute their reporting. What am I supposed to say after I see a profile of Bobby Jones's life that made it very clear he didn't like black people? Am I supposed to say, "God Bless Bobby Jones"?

I was telling some friends that if Tiger keeps winning the Masters, Bobby Jones is gonna walk through the front door of the Augusta National clubhouse one day and say, "If y'all can't beat this colored boy I'm gonna come back from the dead and kick his ass myself. I know y'all can do a better job than this against him."

I know Bobby Jones wasn't alone in the way he thought, but damn, let's not act like a great golfer is the only thing he was. The lives of athletes and public figures get examined all the time today. This ain't the 1930s. Things have to be looked at and discussed and not just swept under the damn rug.

I know people of all colors and ethnic backgrounds, particularly kids and people in their twenties, who don't get bogged down with ugly shit like race; they embrace Tiger. Kids just don't care; they haven't been programmed by adults yet and brainwashed with a whole lot of garbage. Their interests are pure. They see somebody doing something great, they like it and appreciate it and aren't polluted with some sick-ass agenda.

But I think also that a lot of other folks who've been carrying around their own baggage see Tiger win at Augusta and want to think everything is okay. They'll try to act like everything at Augusta National is just fine. Look, if they want to take the easy way out and not confront a whole lot of truths, fine, go ahead. But it's still a bunch of BS.

I didn't know until recently that Lee Trevino went

to that clubhouse only once. Somebody wanted to throw him out the very first time he went there to play and he never wanted to go there again. They made him feel so uncomfortable being there he went out back and changed his shoes. He changed his shoes in the trunk of his car like he was some weekend hacker at a public course. Lee Trevino, one of the greatest golfers of all time. Can you imagine that? And you know there are people running around saying, "How can Lee Trevino be bitter toward Augusta and the Masters?" The people who ask that question, with disgust in their voices, were probably never turned away from someplace or asked to leave or enter a back door because of their color. I was down in Alabama playing golf one day in May, not long after the *Sports Illustrated* article ran, and I ran into some guys who said, "Hale Irwin said your views about Tiger and Augusta National were silly." I said, "Listen, I like Hale Irwin. But Hale Irwin doesn't live in Alabama where y'all are rednecks. Hale Irwin flew in here in a private jet for a few days, maybe a week. He played at the finest country club and he stayed in the most luxurious hotel he could find, which didn't exactly give him a taste of what it's like to be poor and black in Alabama, or poor and white in Alabama for that matter. Of course he's going to feel what I said was silly. But did you ask him if he disagreed with me that blacks and poor whites and Hispanics in this country are treated like shit?" Of course, the guy didn't ask him. He couldn't even connect with the sentiment I was expressing. The larger question would never cross the guy's mind. I'm not saying he was a bad guy. But it simply wouldn't cross his mind.

It's interesting that golf courses are places where guys really talk now. You've got all kinds of people playing together and eating lunch in the clubhouse together, and some of those guys would never meet people different from themselves if it wasn't for the golf course. You've got to think some of the people coming into golf now are there because of Tiger, right? I'm not talking about just black people, but white people and Asian people and Hispanic people who didn't think golf was open to them. A lot of people just started to look at it differently because of him. It's like the game is okay for everybody to participate in.

And a lot of us are always going to remember what we were doing or where we were when he won the Masters for the first time, in 1997, when he just kicked everybody's butt, set the record (270) and the next guy–was it Tom Kite?–was something like 12 strokes back (282). Man, that's a day that changed golf forever. It changed the direction of sports in this country. The day Tiger won, I was playing for the Houston Rockets and we had a Sunday afternoon game. I remember I was nervous as hell. Black people aren't always happy for other black people when they achieve goals, which is something that really bothers me. There's often jealousy involved, and I just don't understand why that is or how something like that got started. But sometimes guys come up to me and say– and they're talking about athletes or entertainers– "Man, you guys have it great." And yeah, the end result is great. But I tell them, "Man, getting there involves some shit you don't want to know about and I don't want to talk about."

But I'm sure that other successful black people, people who have had to negotiate some serious situations to get where they are and appreciate all the BS that comes with trying to climb the mountain, are happy for other successful black people. There's a kinship there because people have gone through similar experiences to achieve something even if their professions aren't the same and don't have much in common. I know successful black people were happy for Tiger in a way that had to be different from people of other races who were happy for Tiger that day, or in awe of what he did. I know black people who do backbreaking work every day of their lives, work like that for forty, fifty years trying to make a better life. But sadly they never get the chance to be successful on a big stage or even on a small stage doing something they love to do. And sometimes they can't completely identify with what some successful black people have gone through just to reach that level.

I looked at Lee Elder, having been the first black man to play in the Masters, with tears in his eyes and I was trying to imagine just how deep his happiness was for Tiger. You know Lee Elder knew better than probably anybody else what Tiger had to go through, and he probably had more of an appreciation for what Tiger did than anybody else. That was so significant to me, just unbelievable. All the brothers in the Houston Rockets locker room that Sunday were just entranced sitting there watching the final round of the Masters. I don't think we knew where we were or what we were doing for those few hours. Tiger had what seemed like a 50-shot lead and stayed perfect on every shot. But we were hanging on every swing and every putt, like he was clinging to a one-shot lead.

You relive it when you're around other people and the topic comes up, Tiger and the Masters. And people who may not feel the same way have asked me, "Why were you so nervous when Tiger had such a big lead and nobody was threatening to challenge him?" And I remind them that this was 1997, one year after Greg Norman lost his final-round lead at the Masters. Every single shot that day, I'm thinking about Greg's collapse the previous year. Man, I almost cried for Greg Norman. It was so hard to watch. Some of my friends at CBS told me Ben Crenshaw broke down and cried watching that. Oh man, that broke my heart that day for that to happen to Greg Norman.

If that had happened to Tiger . . . man . . . I can't even think about it now. It would have been . . . just terrible . . . too terrible to even think about. But it didn't. We couldn't take our eyes off the TV, just sat there and watched every shot, and soaked up every moment of it as if it were happening to one of us. What a great day. That set a whole lot of stuff in motion, didn't it?

If You Don't Win a Championship ...

When Ted Williams passed away in the summer of 2002, it brought about a lot of fascinating reflection and it made me think about how people perceive athletes' careers.

Obviously, in retirement Ted Williams was simply a very good guy. Even though he retired three years before I was born, I appreciated him because of his support for Negro League players who had been banned from playing with him in the major leagues. I've read excerpts of interviews and seen clips of speeches that showed he was about inclusion and integration and recognizing everybody's talents back when baseball didn't want any part of black and Latin players. And even beyond that, in recent times, you knew Ted Williams had to be a really good guy because of the way modern-day players embraced him, and the way he embraced them. The way they surrounded him at that All-Star Game in Boston a few years ago told you how much the people in his profession thought of him.

What's interesting is that in his retirement, when he became the elder statesman of the game, people hardly ever mentioned that he never won a championship with the Red Sox. I had forgotten he hadn't won one until I started reading and watching the obituaries after he died. I mean, I know the Red Sox haven't won a World Series since 1918, and Ted's career went from 1939 to 1960, so obviously he didn't win a World Series. But I'd forgotten about it because nobody tried to diminish him because he hadn't won a World Series. I've read that people brought it up during his career, when he was perceived by a lot of people as being a bad guy, but since he was clearly a good guy for many, many years, people just let it go. It's a serious double standard, and it's silly because it's not like he was two different players. So if he's a good guy it doesn't matter, but if he's a bad guy it does?

Thing is, if Ted Williams had been traded to the Yankees in his rookie year for Joe DiMaggio, Ted would have all those World Series rings and DiMaggio probably wouldn't have had any. But would DiMaggio not have been a great ballplayer? Would Ted have been any better? Ted only played in one World Series, 1946, and the Red Sox lost. But nobody has hit .400 since he did it. The guy won two Triple Crowns, which is almost unthinkable these days. But the bigger point to be made is the perception of what kind of player he was as it relates to playing for a championship team.

It's something that all athletes have to live with, even the guys who win a championship, and it can be frustrating. It obviously hits home with me because I never played on a championship team in my sixteen years in the NBA. Some guy in Los Angeles once wrote that my career wasn't fulfilled because of that. And that's absurd.

Dean Smith once relayed to me a conversation he had with Roy Williams after Dean Smith won his first NCAA Championship, the one where North Carolina beat Georgetown in 1982. People had gotten on Dean Smith about coaching at Carolina for twenty years and not winning the NCAA Championship, even though he'd been to the Final Four a bunch of times. Roy, who was his assistant at the time, said to him as the game ended, "Now you can get 'em off your back about not winning a championship." And Dean Smith said he told Roy, "I'm no better coach now than I was five minutes ago." And it's a great story because it's true, Dean Smith was already a great coach, and because it showed how gracious he was to keep things in perspective even after he won.

But this notion that your career is somehow failed if you don't win a championship, which I think is completely ridiculous, really started to get out of control the last ten years or so. People have just become so critical, so quick to ridicule. Phil Mickelson is going through that right now and I feel bad for him. I know Phil Mickelson. He's the second greatest golfer in the world as I'm writing these words. And I know how badly he wants to win. But I think he's pressing, and unfortunately starting to believe all this stuff about not being able to win a major championship. It's difficult not to because you can't escape it, not with all the sports talk radio and twenty-four-hour sports television and people asking him about it every single tournament. David Duval had it until the summer of 2001 when he won the British Open, and Colin

Montgomerie has it to a degree, but nobody has it like Phil. Well, Greg Norman had it a while back until he won a couple of majors. But even with that, people look back on Greg Norman's career now and you hear them say, "Well, he had the talent to win a lot more majors than he did."

Man, that's flat-out unfair. The people making these assessments for the most part don't have any idea of how difficult it is to win a championship—in golf a major championship—especially if you come along at the same time as the greatest player that sport has ever seen. Of course, I identify with what Phil's going through because I had something very similar.

There's really only one thing wrong with Phil Mickelson: he was born at the wrong time. That's it. He was born too close to Tiger Woods. Same thing happened to me, to Patrick Ewing, John Stockton, Karl Malone, Reggie Miller, a whole bunch of guys. The guys who dominated at the championship level when I played were Earvin Johnson, Larry Bird and Michael Jordan. They won fourteen championships in nineteen seasons. They played in twenty NBA Finals between them. If you want to say that those guys were better than me, I'm going to agree with you. Is there any shame in that?

Once when he was being interviewed Michael gave me a backhanded compliment and said I was on the next level down from him, Larry and Magic. And I called him up and told him I had no problem with that. I told him, "If I'm right after you guys, I'm okay with that." That means I'm with Malone, Stockton, Ewing, Gary Payton. Would I like to have won a championship, several championships? Of course. I played my ass off for sixteen years, trying to win every time out. But don't expect me to see my career as something unfulfilled because I'm with those other guys.

Somebody took a poll once and the question was "Who's the greatest team player in professional sports never to win a championship?" and I was voted No. 1. A similar topic came up when I was on Jim Rome's show once, and I told him, "Jim, you never ask this question of a mediocre player. So I'm taking this as a compliment. When you interview a marginal player who managed to hang in there and last long enough in the league to make himself a ten-year career you tell him, 'You had such a wonderful career.' So by asking me this, you must think I'm a helluva player."

The problem to me is the bar keeps moving. If Phil Mickelson wins a major tournament, but only one, when he retires people will say, "He should have won more." Well, why is that? How many people making this criticism of Phil are the second-best in the world at what they do? You've got a lot of no-talents out there on talk radio running off at the mouth, getting people all riled up when they're not stopping to assess how difficult it is to win a championship in any sport in this day and age, with all the good athletes out there competing. It's still a special thing to win, to even compete for a championship. So I'm telling everybody when they ask me about those guys who didn't win, that it's an honor to be grouped with them. And it is. We're talking about Dan Marino, Jim Kelly, Chris Carter and the NBA guys I just mentioned like Patrick and John Stockton and Karl Malone and Gary Payton. One of the most underappreciated NBA players during my time was Dominique Wilkins. How many people have scored 25,000 points in a career? He was No. 8 all-time in points scored when he retired. But it's not just guys who are my peers who had great careers and didn't win.

Elgin Baylor's knees were so bad late in his career, he wound up retiring before the Lakers won a championship. Ernie Banks never won a World Series, never even played in one. Would anybody be stupid enough to make the case that Ernie Banks's life is unfulfilled, as great an ambassador as he is for the game of baseball? I knew Dick Butkus and Gale Sayers didn't win a Super Bowl, but I didn't know until somebody told me recently that those guys didn't even play a single playoff game in their careers. If you want to make the case that those guys, first-ballot Hall of Fame players, didn't do everything they could while they wore those uniforms, go ahead and try, but it would be pretty stupid.

I cannot imagine that if I won a championship tomorrow I would lie in bed and think, "Oh, I'm complete now." I went out there every night and gave my team everything I had, some nights when I was injured and shouldn't even have been playing. And I know all those other guys did the same thing trying to do whatever they could to help their teams win a championship. We got really close once, in 1993 with Phoenix, and I played on teams that had a chance a couple of other times. I was out there at a little taller than 6-foot-4 battling every night. I think the people I played with and against know that. Only three or four other players retired with more points, rebounds and assists than I had over my career. When I retired, one of my friends wrote me a letter and said, "I've stood beside your short ass and you're only 6-4 but you battled 7-foot guys every night. Congratulations on a wonderful career." That letter meant a lot to me. It was from Quinn Buckner. At the end of several seasons when I was playing, Michael would call me, knowing how disappointed I was, and say, "Hang in there."

That's what really made me angry when Scottie Pippen insulted me and said Michael agreed with him. Michael had just retired and was in Monte Carlo with his family. It was about 2:00 A.M. one night; the story had just broken with Scottie saying all this BS about me. And Michael said, "You know I'd never say that about you. And if I wanted to say it, I'd say it to your face." He didn't need to call me, but it was nice of him to do it.

We all want to win, but not everybody could win, especially not when they had to go through Michael Jordan in the NBA, not when they have to go through the Yankees most of the time in baseball, not when they have to go through Tiger Woods in professional golf. But you go out there and fight the best fight you can fight. It's shameful if you cheat the fans, if you go out there and fail to give everything you've got when they're paying good money to see you. But if you're going to tell me that the twelfth man on one of

Magic's teams or Larry's teams or Michael's teams who played three minutes a night had a more fulfilling career than I did, that's crazy to me. You can't convince me that a guy who caught two passes the whole season on a Super Bowl–winning team had a more fulfilling career than Cris Carter had, or that the third-string quarterback holding a clipboard for a Super Bowl championship team had a more fulfilling career than Dan Marino or Jim Kelly. What you'd be saying then is that there is dishonor in giving your best, being one of the very top guys in your sport, coming close but losing. That's crazy. Those guys didn't win championships either, but they're great at what they did and it's an honor to be mentioned with them.

"I Am Not a
Role Model"

Nike didn't come to me with the idea to do a commercial about role models–I went to Nike with that idea. I talked to my friend the Nike executive Howard White about it, called him after thinking about it for a while, and said, "Howard, people have this role model thing completely screwed up. Is a role model just a celebrity that parents turn their kids over to? Damn, can't we do better than that? Is the best we can do for kids pointing them to celebrities they have no real chance of ever knowing?" I just thought we as a society need to do better in that area. So I asked, and Nike said, cool. And I thought it turned out great.

Remember, the main theme was "I am not a role model."

And for that, I got ripped. I'd been criticized before, of course, for having my own take on social issues. But the first time I got hit really hard was for taking that stance. There were some columnists who defended me, but mostly I got killed. I'm okay with it, though, because nobody in all this time has been able to convince me that it's wrong to tell kids to listen to their parents and not a basketball player they've never met. How crazy is it to get slammed for saying, "Listen to your parents, listen to your teachers, listen to the responsible adults in your neighborhood or people who have done something with their lives." I know it's hard to get an entire message across in less than a minute. But I still believe the message was clear enough that I thought kids need to be able to look up to folks right there around them who can teach them hard work and right from wrong.

Celebrities can't teach 'em that from television. People are crazy. Or maybe they're just lazy, they don't want to do the hard work, and it's easier to just turn their kids over to somebody 'cause he's famous. How stupid is that? How can you make somebody your role model when you don't know the person?

All they've got most of the time is a perception of somebody off in the distance that might be totally distorted . . . or it could be the person is just misunderstood. One thing I hate is that all the general public knows about an athlete or a celebrity is what they know from the media, which is often inaccurate or incomplete. I know cases where a guy is labeled a bad guy and he's really a good guy, maybe worthy of being a role model for kids he's close to. And I know of way too many instances where the guy comes off as a good guy in the media and he's not a good guy at all. And that's a huge problem. Either way, how could that person be a legitimate role model for a kid? Because he's famous? Because he's on TV? Can he help get questions answered for you or do anything that's specific to what you need?

Television is entertainment. I love television. And in this second stage of my life it pays me well. But television is entertainment, television is celebrity. And with so few people to emulate in their neighborhoods, black kids started fantasizing about being athletes. And having dreams is great, but how can somebody on TV help give you any direction? That's a one-way relationship. A ballplayer you can only see on TV may inspire you to do great things in athletics, sure. You can look at sports all day and want to try and do things on a court or a field like that player. But that can't help you with your homework, or with real aspirations, or help you if you're having problems at home. How does an athlete help you if you're a terrible athlete but a decent student and you need encouragement to compete academically?

A role model should be among the people who can influence your direction in a real-life way. The best scenario is if they can be actually in your life. My mother and grandmother were my two biggest role models; my dad wasn't there. It was my mother and grandmother. A role model, in my way of thinking, is somebody who can help shape your life and what you believe in. And it can't be somebody on television, somebody you can't touch or go to for advice, or cuss you out when it's necessary or sit and listen to you. It may be more important to have mentors than role models anyway, maybe somebody you can talk to about stuff you may not feel comfortable talking to your parents about. It needs to be somebody who's not going to tell you exactly what you want to hear all the time.

At the time, I felt I needed to attack the subject because on the whole I don't think athletics are good for black kids. I really don't. I got to this point because every single time I go and talk to black children or teenagers at a school or at an event, they only want to play sports. I'll ask them what they want to do after high school or about their plans in the next few years and it's always "I want to play pro basketball" or "I want to play in the NFL." Every single one, it seems to me, wants to play sports for a living. It's like there's some mental block, or they've been conditioned or brainwashed to feel they can't do anything but play sports. And it's scary to me. It bothers me. Obviously, I'm not against sports; I'm thankful for everything a career in professional sports has given me. But I don't know of any other culture where the children all want to do the same thing. I've never heard of any other situation like that.

I know this is complex and there are some real contradictions here because the most really influential group of black people in America is made up of a lot of athletes. There aren't any Martin Luther Kings or Malcolm Xs or Medgar Everses leading the black community right now. Almost everybody, among the most prominent people in our communities right now, who has achieved any status the past twenty-five years has done so through athletics, which in a way is really a shame. We have a lot of hardworking people, folks doing backbreaking work. But we still don't see the doctors and lawyers and engineers we need to see and need to have portrayed and need to treat as role models. And the ones we do have don't have any real platform. They're not doing anything controversial enough or scandalous enough to get profiles in the mainstream magazines. Athletes and entertainers are the only ones among us who have the platform, mostly because they're on television every day.

So when you seriously start to think about it, our kids are so limited in the number of successful black people they can see or be exposed to. They see athletes and entertainers and what else? How often do they see scientists and engineers and writers? They don't. I know in my own neighborhood, I didn't know any black doctors or lawyers or professional black folks. They weren't in the projects where I grew up. I know a whole lot of these kids I'm talking to come from neighborhoods that ain't all that different from mine.

I'm not saying that poor white kids and Hispanic kids don't have similar issues with this, because I suspect they do, too. And I'm not saying that only professional people can be role models. A guy working the nine-to-five cleaning the streets or running the grocery store on the corner could be a great role model. You need to see honest, hardworking people and appreciate what they're doing with their lives. And just because somebody doesn't have a college degree doesn't mean he or she can't help give some direction to a kid who can't get it anywhere else. But we also need our kids to see some professional people they can aspire to be like, and they don't see enough. Every kid can't be Michael Jordan or Will Smith, and shouldn't want to be. But this is what they see in their lives every day, because for so many of them they ain't got anything positive going on at home.

Anyway, this had been bothering me for a while and I wanted to use my own platform to address it. And I never thought so many people would miss the bigger message. I found it interesting in the spring of 2002 that somebody came up with this TV campaign: "Parents, the anti-drug." Isn't that the same point I was making in the role model commercial? That campaign is a damn good reminder. But it's nothing different from what I was saying in the role model commercial. What's different about it? It doesn't say, "Athletes and celebrities, the anti-drug," does it? I wasn't supposed to have any ideas of my own or talk about anything serious?

All I was saying was your parents and your teachers, people you ought to be listening to, need to be your role models. Charles Barkley the basketball player should not be your role model. Yeah, I can be a role model to my daughter and to kids I have some contact with. But that's not only Charles Barkley the basketball player, that's me as a father, or a parental figure. Those kids don't see me only on TV, there's an actual relationship there, or at least some association. How many people on TV do these kids have an association with? We all know the answer is "None."

But if it took me getting slammed to get some dialogue started on this issue, then it was worth it. I'd do it again in a second.

Making a Difference . . . Politics and Business

Politics seem like such a scam sometimes, because our system is supposed to be inclusive and it's supposed to represent everybody, right? Okay, so how many black U.S. senators are there? There are no black or Hispanic governors, even though black and Hispanic people make up about 20 percent of the population in the United States. You have to wonder if making an impact is easier to do through private enterprise than it is working through politics in a lot of cases. I'm not saying we shouldn't try to do it through the political process because we should, of course. But look at Earvin Johnson, for example. He's making

a difference. Look at the impact he's had since he retired from his playing career. He's partnered with
Starbucks to go into communities that would never
otherwise have a Starbucks. And not only did he put a
brand-new Starbucks in the 'hood, he took a Borders
Books in there, a Subway sandwich shop. He's got
movie theaters in several cities. All those businesses
represent full-time jobs, part-time jobs. They represent hope, too. A lot of these communities don't have
anybody investing in them. They're just forgotten
communities. I know in some of those cases there
was nothing there but vacant buildings or some
empty strip mall. I've read where each one of his Starbucks is one of the top-grossing stores in the whole
country.

I can't say enough about how proud I am of
Earvin and what he's doing.

See, this is part of my disagreement with Jim
Brown. Earvin has done this since retiring. That's
what I'm trying to do now in retirement: find the best
way to make an impact and improve people's lives. I
don't think you can devote enough time to these types
of efforts and do it properly while you're still playing.
A playing career now is a full-time job. Yeah, we get
some downtime and some vacation time. But it's not

like it was in the 1960s when the NFL season was twelve games and the NBA playoffs ended in early May, and guys went out and got jobs in the off-season because their sport lasted only half the year. These days, the club owns your ass almost year-round.

To be fair, we can never know all the stuff guys in Jim Brown's era went through and the battles they had to fight and frustrations they had. If you're in your thirties or forties you can only imagine what it was like, so I understand what he's calling for. I don't know what it was like to have to stay in a separate hotel from my teammates or have to enter the back door of a restaurant to eat in certain cities. I understand why he wants people to be active socially. He was involved in a lot of stuff from what I can tell. And he still is.

But we can only fight the battles that we are presented with now. Earvin is doing a tremendous job. People say they don't see famous black athletes using their platform, using their influence to impact change. Jim Brown has said that about today's athletes. But again, look at Earvin. You think a poor white or poor black person could have gone to the chairman of Starbucks and said, "Hey, man, I want to start putting Starbucks in urban neighborhoods where they don't have any coffee shops." He couldn't even get his call through.

Earvin is using his celebrity and his wealth to do something serious as an entrepreneur. There's so much pressure on black athletes today, black famous people period. And I hope people can use their stature to make a difference. But if a guy does that, give him credit. Maybe people will get some inspiration from what Earvin is doing.

There are various ways to go about it. People ask me all the time, "Charles, are you going to run for governor of Alabama? Are you going to run next term?" And I say, "That's next year!" I just retired. I'm relaxing now, enjoying myself, trying to figure out what life holds for me. There are a lot of things I want to do, and I have to identify the important ones and identify what I've got the best chance to get done. I do know I want to help rebuild downtown Birmingham, which is essentially vacant. I'm trying to help rebuild my hometown, Leeds. I've been meeting with people for the last two, three months and it's interesting that none of those people are closely involved in politics.

It's more daunting for the simple fact that you think you can run for public office and you have this enormous power. But unless you're part of the larger process with a state legislature, it doesn't mean any-thing. That's the thing that's caught me off guard the most, how many people you have to have moving in the same direction with you. If you don't have that army of people, what you do is irrelevant.

This past spring and summer, I had some weeks where I had two and three meetings a day with home builders, community planners. There are some ways, I believe, to help bring about some serious changes that don't have anything to do with the political pro-cess. One of the things I have to figure out is, do I want to pursue a job with one-tenth the money, 1,000 times the stress and aggravation 365 days a year? I had a resident of Alabama come up to me the other day and say, "Please run for governor." And I said, "Hey, slow your roll. Let me do some things over the next few years that let people know my heart is in the right place. Let me be involved in this effort to rebuild parts of Alabama. Let me take some small steps first." It's important to me, because without economic opportu-nity, all this other talk is irrelevant. I can talk about all the grand plans in the world, but until we do some-thing about a school system that's tens of million's of dollars in debt it's just a lot of talk. Let me see if I can help attract some businesses to move into our state, so we can increase the tax base. There used to be a Parisians, a Sears, those types of big huge stores. But now they've moved. They're not downtown anymore. I'm not saying Birmingham is the only place where this has happened, but Alabama is my home, so this is close to me. There's a community called Hoover which is like our own little Buckhead. There are beautiful developments all around it, which is great. But the businesses left the downtown area, and now we've got too damn many vacant buildings and the downtown isn't viable anymore.

I've just started getting involved, but the support has been phenomenal. I think the business and political leaders at home want to do better. They've been beat down for so long, the image of the state is so poor. But you know what? The image of the state is deserved. We always say, "Thank God for Mississippi and Arkansas or we'd be dead last in everything."

I'm not about to rule out politics. But I don't know yet how it's going to turn out. The National Republican Black Caucus sent guys from Alabama and guys from D.C. to talk to me back in April. I understand how the game works. They want me to be involved. They need black Republicans in Alabama. President Bush wants to use me in different ways nationally. I understand and appreciate that. I want to play the game. But the party has to give to get. I'm not a dummy. They've got certain issues they want addressed and need addressed. And I've got certain needs I'd like to see met, like refurbishing my hometown, Leeds, and downtown Birmingham, which are both ghost towns now.

Leeds is the story of every small town. When Wal-Mart went up across town, so many of the small businesses went away. It's a complete ghost town. I'm serious about this. I'm not going to let them not take me seriously. Whatever I do next should start at home. I'm not looking for anything for myself. We've got a lot of black people, poor white people and Hispanic people who need the playing field leveled, who need jobs. They just need a chance, a job, a place to start. The school system in Alabama is so far in debt. That situation has to improve. It's great that we just got Hyundai and Mercedes-Benz. But new businesses got $700 million in tax cuts, barely paid taxes for twenty years. Rich folks gave away so much money that was intended for poor people.

The South is still such a good ol' boy network–still is–that if you have any influence or any standing you need to stand up and be counted. I guess I could just keep my TV job, make a couple of million a year and be happy. But there's no way God allowed me to make all this money, meet all the people I've met and rise to this status just to sit around, count my money and not try to help people improve their lives.

These are some of the things I talked with the Republican Black Caucus guys about. I'm not going to be a token. They talk about all these appearances they want me to make, because there are a lot of big elections coming up, particularly in Alabama, where the gubernatorial election is in November. I said I'll meet with the candidates and see what they're talking about.

I was asked for years about being a Republican, probably because most black people are Democrats. My mother heard it once and called me and said, "Charles, Republicans are for the rich people." And I said, "Mom, I'm rich." But the workings of politics are so strange that I've decided in recent months not to be worried about party affiliation as much as about trying to help the best candidates get things done, and that may involve being independent and keeping my options open.

I think the biggest misconception is that the Democratic Party does so much to help poor people. In a whole lot of cases the Democratic Party keeps people poor. Just about every single person in my hometown is a Democrat. And they are living exactly the same way they lived when I left there twenty years ago. Their lives have not been financially improved in any substantial way in all that time. My high school, Leeds High School, is closing. And the whole area has been vacated. Their lives are not any better.

I asked my mother and grandmother about why things never got any better under the politicians that ran things for so many years, and they kept voting for 'em. And they'd say, "We're Democrats." And I'd say, "Why? All these people vote this way every single election and things are still the same." What did they do in exchange for all that loyalty for all those years? I don't see any new economic opportunities in my hometown. You have to go to Birmingham to get a job. Part of what initially attracted me to the Republican Party is that I see—whether I'm right or wrong—what the Democratic Party has not done where I'm from.

Since then, I've gotten to meet and know some of the important Republican leaders. Living in Arizona, I got a chance to get to know John McCain. People act like Republicans haven't had a full range of life experiences. I think McCain's seen it all. The guy earned a

Purple Heart, he was a prisoner of war, he relates to all kinds of people. I think he probably got slapped around a little bit in the last presidential election. A lot of people really liked him, his platform and the issues he campaigned on. But the Republican Party said, "Hey, George Bush is going to be the guy." I bet he was probably a bit disillusioned. In fact, he was totally disillusioned after the election. Money changes a lot of things.

People ask me if politics will ever excite me like sports. The answer is no. Absolutely not, no way. There's nothing that can excite you like sports. Athletic competition is its own rush. But after you have to stop competing in sports, there are other areas where competing can help a whole lot of people who need help, and business and politics are two of them.

Home and Away

One of the great benefits of making a career out of professional sports is the travel. On the most basic level, road trips are business trips: you're going to a place in order to make your living, a place that you probably wouldn't be visiting otherwise. But once you're there, it can be so educational and rewarding if you only allow yourself to experience the people and the culture.

One of the cool things about travel is finding places you want to visit over and over again when you hit town. If you're going to Milwaukee, you've got to go to Perkins, the soul food spot. There's another spot

I love in Phoenix, Johnson's. Houston is one of the best restaurant cities in America, maybe the most underrated. A spot named Ruggles is one of my favorites. South Philly has a ton of great restaurants.

I've also found living in different places–Philadelphia when I first left Alabama, then Phoenix and then Houston–fascinating. Take Philadelphia. Philadelphia is just a real tough city. A lot of people in the news media can make it difficult to play there because a bad game or a bad series isn't treated as a bad game or a bad series. It's treated as though you're a bad guy and you meant to play poorly, like you're personally trying to cheat the team and the fans. Even if you're a star player it can be difficult to live in Philly because of that. And if you think you can separate living in a place from how you're treated publicly, you're crazy.

Now, I know the fans can be tough, too. But I always thought the fans treated me great. And that's not to say that there weren't some tough nights and difficult stretches. But overwhelmingly, I thought the fans were great to me. And what I find really interesting is that once I was traded, after playing in Philly for eight years, the fans showed how much they appreciated me when I returned for games. From what I could see, the same was true for Randall Cunningham once he was traded from the Eagles after a great run, and would come back to town to play against them. It seemed to me as if, regardless of what had happened before, the fans tried to really show Randall they appreciated all the effort he put forth to help make that team a contender every week for years.

But when it does go sour, it really goes sour. When it does, I think it's largely because a columnist or talk show host or somebody prominent in the local media puts the hammer on somebody, and then the fans just run with it and it becomes a huge local issue that just hangs around for days and weeks. When Eric Lindros first arrived in Philadelphia to play for the Flyers, I was playing golf with him and I told him early on, "Eric, you have to watch your back. This can be a really enjoyable city but it can also be very tough and you have to know that going in."

He was just a kid at the time, and he thought, "Hey, this is going to be okay." And I understand that, because you can't know another city until you experience it, until you know what the people are like and what makes them tick, what gets them inflamed. And it's very hard to appreciate how frustrated fans might be about a certain team's performance historically. I do know that about five years later, I saw

Eric someplace and he said, "Man, you were so right years ago." See, when things go bad, they really go bad.

I will say this, though I know a lot of people in Philly will see it as criticism: They were wrong to boo Kobe Bryant the way they did at the 2002 All-Star Game in Philly. It was ugly, mean and totally unwarranted. From what I understand, the people who have a beef with Kobe in Philly are upset that he said going into the 2001 NBA Finals that he wanted to come back and "cut Philly's heart out." He was referring to the 76ers, not the city of Philadelphia, and everybody should have been able to see that. The context was clear to me. And for that, people booed him unmercifully. But what else is he supposed to say when he's playing against the 76ers for the NBA championship? You expect him to say, "We'll come there and have a big love fest"? You'd better have the attitude that you're going to cut another team's heart out when you're playing for the biggest prize in your profession. In 1993, I wanted to cut the Bulls' heart out, even though I love the city of Chicago. To feel anything less would be disappointing to me. To boo a player that great, when he's from the town where you live, and he's never done anything to embarrass himself or his family or his city, that's just not right, I don't care what anybody says.

So, yeah, when things go bad for a guy in Philly they really go bad. Scott Rolen of the Philadelphia Phillies found that out the hard way in the summer of 2002. Once he turned down a contract extension, it was just a matter of time until they ran him out of there because so many guys in the press and people in Phillies management treated that as a personal rejection of them. And then the fans run with it, and all of a sudden it's just miserable. When the work environment is difficult, living wherever you live is going to be difficult, no matter how wonderful the city is, especially when you're living a public life.

The sad thing is sometimes you don't really get to enjoy a city the first few years you're there simply because making friends is so difficult. There are just too many balls to juggle at one time. You're trying to find a place to live in a community you know nothing about. You're trying to learn a new city. You're trying to practice and play as well as you can as a rookie, or as a guy just signed or traded to a new team. You have new teammates to learn and adjust to. And half the time, you're not even there, because you're traveling.

Obviously, though, I think the fans in Philadelphia

have been great to me, and it was a great place for me to be those eight years, because I still live part of the year in the Philly area. My first culture shock was coming to Philly from Alabama. I had my first cheese-steak my first or second day there. I didn't like it. There was too much meat and it was messy. It just wasn't my thing. So that was my one and only cheese-steak. But that's one of the few things in Philly that disagreed with me: I met a lot of wonderful people there.

And the turning point of my adult life came in Philly. Winning had become so important, so consuming, that it was okay in my mind at the time to spit on a heckler. By now many people know the story, that I missed the guy I was spitting at and hit a little girl named Lauren Rose who was attending the game that night and sitting near the heckler. The thing that really struck me the most when I talked to Lauren two days later was her demeanor, how calm she was, how nice and trusting. I haven't talked to her in a while, but she and her parents were such nice people. I knew then and there I would never do anything like that again. There are things that happen in the heat of battle with players, but they're combatants in that arena with you. There's *nothing* that should make you do what I did that night. I told myself, "Calm your ass *down.*" That's the one thing I really, really regret.

My second culture shock came when I was traded to Phoenix before the 1992–93 season. Being from Leeds, Alabama, and living my first eight years in Philly, I had never in my life had much contact with a large Hispanic community or Hispanic culture. So I got there, and obviously the Phoenix metropolitan area has a large Hispanic population, and it was eye-opening for me.

The people I met in the Hispanic communities in Arizona were incredibly hardworking. They'd come to a new place, where the language was a second language, and their mission was to educate their children and make their families' lives better and be able to enjoy both their own culture and the mainstream culture in America. It makes me so damn angry to hear people say, "We've got too many immigrants coming into the country," as if that's the biggest problem we have.

The Hispanic people I met came into a new country, did the most menial jobs in a lot of cases, took whatever work they could get without bitching or complaining, and did everything with honor and pride. And sometimes you have to wonder if the economy might collapse without them taking some of the jobs they take, and gradually accumulating something for themselves. A whole lot of people who've been in America for generations could do the same thing if they didn't consider it beneath them.

When I was living in Philly, for those five winter months it was pretty much just going from practice to home, games and back home, the airport and back home. It was cold out and I was pretty much locked down indoors from November through March. But I got to Phoenix, and suddenly I could wear shorts to practice, play golf after practice, get outdoors and experience mountains and desert. But to have a whole new culture to be introduced to was for me an entirely different thing. Wherever you live, it's about the people in the end.

.   .   .

I can't imagine my life without travel. It's just cool to go to so many different places. Growing up in Alabama, in a segregated environment where the black people lived on one side of town and the white people lived on another, there was a tense feeling about everyone different—folks didn't like blacks, didn't like Jews, didn't like Yankees, didn't like foreigners. And to travel—and I was lucky enough to do it when I was young–is to experience that the country can be better than that, and the world can be better than that.

I don't know that I would want to live in Portland, but it's a great town. And the fans make it probably the best place to play in the NBA. I imagine it would be a great place to play an entire career because the people are so welcoming. I loved going to old Chicago Stadium. It was so intimate and loud and the people were right up on top of you. The Chicago Stadium and Boston Garden certainly had their similarities, but they were mean at Boston Garden. The people in Chicago always seemed to have a real affection for me when I went there. It was probably because of my relationship with Michael Jordan. When Michael's father was murdered in 1993, he asked me if I would host his golf tournament in suburban Chicago. I did, and that just seemed to make my relationship with people in Chicago even warmer.

I hate all the new arenas, although I never played in the new building in Indiana. But these new arenas are just too big, they're filled with luxury suites because of the owners' greed. The fans are much too far away from the action. They're nothing like the old Chicago Stadium and the old building in Portland, Memorial Coliseum. Those were great buildings.

Domestic travel is a big part of your life because you're playing forty-one road games a year plus play-off road games. But there's plenty of opportunity for international travel, which is hands down to me the most educational thing you can do. For my first ten years in the NBA, Nike put together international trips. The first couple of times I went on these trips, I figured we could be pretty anonymous. When you're young and you've never been anywhere really, you just don't think anybody overseas knows who you are. Then we'd go to Germany or France and have thousands of people come to exhibition games.

I was never worried about language differences. They weren't barriers, they were just differences. You could still communicate despite the differences. Probably, Germany and Japan have been my two favorite countries to visit, although I did go back to Spain two or three times since the 1992 Olympics in Barcelona. A lot of people have made a big deal out of me walking around Barcelona in '92 and mingling with people. To me, one of the great things in life is to get out and meet new people, people whose experiences are different from your own. It has nothing to do with being recognized and well known. To me, that's what you're supposed to do, get out and enjoy a new city.

I loved Barcelona. Loved it. Maybe some people don't enjoy doing that, but I do. I know there are times I've been walking around a city overseas, 10,000 miles from home, and I've thought, "Here I am, this little kid from Leeds, Alabama, and I'm in Barcelona . . . or Paris . . . or Tokyo."

At the same time, though, I've been riding around in one of those cities and been through a neighborhood where the houses on a particular street looked exactly like the houses on a street back home. Parts of Munich, to me, looked exactly like parts of New York City. Germany might be the country I'm most surprised about liking so much. I just didn't know what to expect, knowing what we know about the atrocities of World War II. . . . You just don't know a place until you go and see for yourself.

One of the things I find different about Europe is that the people tend to honor their athletes. There seems to be a different relationship between the people and athletes. And one of the things I really like is when you walk down the street and interact with people, nobody's trying to borrow money, and there's no player hating. I've been asked if my enjoyment of international travel is enhanced by being well known internationally, and if as a black American I'm treated

differently. And it's difficult for me to answer that because I didn't travel before I became so recognizable.
You'd be naive if you think people don't react differently to you because in their eyes you're a celebrity.
But I'll say this: even when people haven't known me
overseas, there's a lack of what I perceive as the racial
tension you feel when you're at home in a lot of different parts of America. I don't have a definitive answer as to why that seems to be the case, and there
are probably a thousand reasons for it. Mostly, I think
it's just ignorance, and that causes the tension. It's ignorance tension. But I don't dwell on it, I just try to
enjoy people wherever I am because what travel
should teach anyone is that people can socialize and
relate and rise above the tension. I really feel bad for
the people who never get the opportunity to broaden
their horizons, take themselves out of a place that's
limited. So many people just have no chance to do
that.

Obviously, there are differences whenever you go
to a new country, or even a new city, and that's what
makes it so appealing in the first place, being able to
experience something that's not like what you have at
home or eat at home or do culturally at home. But ultimately, we're more the same than not. I don't see

that as a contradiction. Anything that's going to hold your attention is probably going to be complex and include contradictions. Travel reminds you of that, too, that the similarities between us, the ways we're all kind of the same, are as fascinating as the differences.

A Unique Fraternity

Being a professional athlete puts you in a unique fraternity. To me it's the greatest fraternity in the world. When bad things happen to an athlete—it could be a baseball player or football player, doesn't matter—particularly in championship-level competition, my heart just breaks. People forget what a great baseball player Bill Buckner was and what a great career he had. They focus on one ground ball error in the World Series. There's nothing worse than when you're on that island by yourself and millions and millions of people are watching and you screw up. It's a horrible thing. Nobody's going to hand you a blanket; there's no cover to put over yourself. You're standing in the middle of the field or court—which at that time feels like the middle of the whole world—and everybody's watching and you've just got to gather yourself and get through it.

The person watching at home probably hasn't been in that kind of situation. Until you've been in it you can't know what it's like. Sometimes the tension is running so high you can't breathe out there. And it ain't like the guy is out there trying to screw up, but you're just out there as tight as a drum.

I've heard guys say in certain circumstances they literally had trouble breathing. I was a bad SOB in my day, and I always felt like pressure was fun. Some guys got uncomfortable when they knew everybody was watching some big national TV game. I always felt like, "Good, everybody's gonna watch me kick these guys' ass and there's nothing they can do about it." So I had never really felt pressure before in my life. But Game 1 in the NBA Finals against the Bulls, I looked around the locker room and everybody had *That Look*. And I said, "Oh, shit." I had never seen that before. My team was so terrified in the Finals. I was thinking we could beat the Bulls in the 1993 NBA Finals, that we had home court, all we had to do was get these first couple of games. Of course, we lost the first two, and all three games we played at home.

• • •

One of the things I don't understand, and one of the things that bothers me, is young athletes not paying homage to the people who came before them. The people who came along earlier created a situation or environment that the guys who came along later wanted to be a part of, right?

I'm going to pay homage to Bill Russell. And for a whole lot of reasons. First, he was a better player than me. Second, and this is a personal reason, the black players forty years ago were playing in such a difficult environment. Now, you know Michael Jordan is my best friend. But he shouldn't have been voted the No. 1 athlete of the twentieth century in the ESPN *Sports-Century* poll because I don't think any black athlete today has to deal with what black athletes endured twenty-five, fifty, a hundred years ago. If you had to deal with all that overt prejudice and bigotry and still managed to become a champion in your sport, how much does that say about you? I don't think we can imagine how much garbage those guys put up with just to have a chance to compete in their sports. Imagine if they were just free to play ball and not deal with all the other shit that caused stress and sucked the energy and life out of them? We can't even imagine having to fight just to find a hotel that would let you stay there, or a restaurant that would let you eat there. Michael never had to play with people screaming "Nigger!" as he shot a free throw.

Joe Louis, Jackie Robinson, Josh Gibson, Muhammad Ali, the early black players in the NFL . . . I feel Michael Jordan is the greatest basketball player, but to say Michael's greater than those guys is just bullshit. People are talking about Hank Aaron a little bit more these days, but for the most part I don't think people know a fraction of the shit Hank Aaron went through, and we're talking about the 1970s, not the 1940s. Hank Aaron got so much hate mail, so many death threats as he approached Babe Ruth's home run record. I don't know how he hit any damn home runs in those years. I don't know how he kept it all together.

And I'm supposed to sit here now and believe that today's athletes, black or white, have to perform under conditions as difficult as the ones Hank Aaron had to perform under? Hank's a living legend to me. I was glad to see Kobe Bryant wearing Hank's Atlanta Braves jersey during the NBA Finals last summer, just to put Hank into our consciousness again. Maybe it caused some kids who don't really know anything about him to ask their parents or look him up on the Internet. Why is Hank Aaron treated as just another great ballplayer? If Babe Ruth is a god for what he accomplished—and Babe Ruth earned everything he got—then shouldn't Aaron be approaching that status since he broke Ruth's record? I always found it amazing that Joe DiMaggio wouldn't go to any baseball event unless he was introduced as "The Greatest Living Ballplayer." Can you imagine if a black ballplayer said, "I'm not appearing anywhere, I'm not going to any old-timers games, unless I'm referred to as 'The Greatest Living Ballplayer'"? He'd be tarred and feathered.

I just get upset when guys who have made significant contributions to sports and society are forgotten. How can anybody drawing a paycheck in sports today not know about Curt Flood? He's one of my heroes, and he gets lost in sports history, Curt Flood. He's never gotten an appropriate amount of credit. How did his contributions get so overlooked? Athletes had no say in where they played until Curt Flood stood up and refused to be traded. How can he not be a bigger figure in the modern history of sports? Unless you make a conscious effort to find something on Curt Flood, you won't hear his name, and that's really sad.

We spend so much time concentrating on junk when there are admirable people involved in sports, really nice people who make significant contributions. Three of the nicest people I've ever met in my life are Emmitt Smith, Wayne Gretzky and Mario Lemieux. Carl Lewis is great. You know who I'm really impressed with? Mike Krzyzewski. When he was on the Olympic coaching staff, I spent a lot of time picking his brain. I made a conscious decision to sit down and talk with him every day, and I'm just really impressed with him. And as I've said, the guys who were the most influential in my life were Julius Erving and Moses Malone. I can't tell you how important it was to have them as mentors when I was young and just coming into the league.

One thing we all share–and some guys deal with this better than others–is that no matter how hard you work at your craft and no matter how successful you become, people just have to find something negative to hang on you. You can be the greatest ever at what you do, and people will still turn on you. Even with all the championships Michael Jordan has won, people say, "Well, he's a great basketball player but he's not socially conscious." Now we're hearing the same thing about Tiger. Phil Mickelson has to hear that he hasn't won any majors, then when he wins a couple it'll be that he should have won more. The bar is always being raised as you go. The rules are always being rewritten.

There's aggravation that comes with that, but that's part of what makes triumph so sweet.

Television and Hollywood

Rudy Martzke, the sports television critic for *USA Today*, tried to start something one night down on the set at Turner in Atlanta. He said, "Charles, you didn't win an Emmy." I told him I didn't care about stuff like that, and I meant it. I couldn't be happier that Ernie Johnson won an Emmy. And I'm really glad our show won an Emmy. I'm not stupid. If the show never won an Emmy before now, and they add me to the mix and we won an Emmy, I helped contribute to an Emmy-winning show. I had something to do with it, and that's enough.

We do have great chemistry, and we have a good time while trying to give some insight as to what happened or what people should look for in a game, or around the league, or in the next couple of weeks. I think Kenny disagrees with me sometimes just to disagree, but I really, really like Kenny. And I love Ernie. The guy is a real professional and he and Kenny make it very comfortable for guests to sit on the set and participate in discussions on live TV, which can scare some guys. And in my case, I think it works because Turner allows me to have fun with it, and for us to have fun with each other.

People wonder why I went with Turner and not NBC. But I studied both shows, and I just didn't think NBC was going to let me have fun the way I wanted to have fun. I know that a network like NBC has a certain way it wants to treat the product, and I understand that. But to me, the product is entertainment, and if you don't entertain people it's not going to work. The powers-that-be in sports made it a business, and that business is entertainment. Only one team wins the championship. Some teams have no chance to contend for the championship at all, but they better entertain people for an entire season, make 'em happy and keep 'em wanting to come to the games, or at least watch the games on TV, or they're going out of business.

What I like is trying to find a way to be entertaining, but also tackle some tough issues. I hate when television doesn't want to tackle tough issues, but just make all the money and avoid getting real out of fear. To me, that's a disservice. I guess the secret is finding a way to entertain and make people comfortable enough so that they'll stay tuned in when you do take a stand on real issues. I'm not saying it's easy or that we should do it all the time, but damn, don't you have a responsibility to try?

I could do my thing, make my money, go play golf and be happy, but is that all it's supposed to be about? There aren't that many black people in positions of power or influence. Especially on TV. And if you don't use that position to speak up, it's a wasted position.

I like doing TV, but in the second season I started to feel some negative vibes. In the first year I got all these plaudits for being honest and straightforward. But if you check the tapes I was talking mostly about basketball. I was doing pretty straight analysis. I didn't stray too far that first season. I didn't want to come in right away and start taking on certain social issues, even if they did relate to sports and specifically basketball. I figured I'd just take it easy and I got all this great feedback, I mean really great publicity. It was fun.

But this year I made a conscious decision to see where everybody was coming from. I talked one night about Michael Jordan and Tiger and what in the world it is people expect of them. And when I made that comment that Bobby Jones was probably rolling over in his grave after Tiger won his third Masters Green Jacket, people got a little uncomfortable. They were uncomfortable with me—but not with the fact that Bobby Jones was a bigot.

Somebody asked me about Notre Dame hiring Tyrone Willingham and how it represented progress. And my response was, "You're asking me if it's a big deal for any school to be hiring a black coach in 2002? That's disgraceful." I can't believe any school would try to act like it's doing a proven black coach a favor just to hire him. Didn't ESPN do an entire *Outside the Lines* on that issue? In 2002, this is still a big deal? You've got to be kidding me. I just started saying what I feel, especially when it comes to the big issues of the day in sports. I hope people aren't expecting me to just talk about so-and-so scoring 20 points when there's real issue stuff going on. If you're not going to deal with any significant subjects, what's the point?

I enjoy trying to find that balance between addressing issues and entertaining. Most days, I think the media has the easiest job in the world, because funny stuff happens every day. I was riding the stationary bike one morning in a health club in Atlanta the day of a Turner broadcast. I was watching some program which was showing clips of all the funny stuff comedians said about Robert Blake. Man, he took a beating. . . . He deserved to take a beating 'cause indications are he killed somebody. Come on, now. He ate at that restaurant two days a week for twenty-five years, and that was the first time he ever took his wife? First time in twenty-five years? Guy went there so much the restaurant named an entrée after him. If you can't get off some funny lines about Robert Blake, man, you shouldn't even have been on the air.

You know the thing I want never to get caught up in? Ratings. I have zero respect for the ratings because I don't know anybody who has a Nielsen box in his house. I ask people all the time when the subject of TV comes up, "Do you know anybody who has a Nielsen box at home?" I know a million people. How come I don't know anybody who knows anybody who has a damn Nielsen box? How is that possible?

Sometimes I'll find the ratings in the newspaper for the previous week and it'll say some show was No. 1 and I'll sit there and think, "We ain't watching that!" I know they're not taking any polls in the ghetto.

The two shows I think are the best shows on television are *The Practice* and *Boston Public.* They've got diverse casts. They've got story lines that make you think. They've got a point of view. And they're definitely entertaining. Now, *Friends* is a show I never watched. I like Jerry Seinfeld as a guy. I think he's funny. But I never watched *Seinfeld* when it was on in prime time. I watch it a lot of days now in syndication because my daughter watches it. But I don't believe the ratings, and one of the reasons is that black folks and Hispanics lead the way in watching TV. They must not be measuring in the 'hood. In fact, I've met a lot of people over the years, and I've never met anyone who has a Nielsen box.

I know the ratings for golf have skyrocketed since Tiger came on the scene. But I'm saying if they took ratings in the 'hood the golf ratings when Tiger plays would be even higher because ain't a black person I know who doesn't build his weekend around watching Tiger play.

When I was growing up, I watched *Good Times, Sanford and Son, The Jeffersons, Gunsmoke, What's Happening!!* Every black person in America, as far as I could tell, watched *The Cosby Show.* I know it was No. 1 in the ratings, but I'd bet the show was watched by so many more people than the Nielsen ratings suggested because it isn't surveying the 'hood. Okay, people will say, "Charles is being paranoid." Hasn't it been proven that blacks and Hispanics have been consistently undercounted in the U.S. census? Wasn't that a major point of the 2000 census, to make sure poor people were counted properly? Damn, how hard is it to find black and Hispanic people? Most of 'em are living in the biggest cities in the damn country. The census takers just didn't want to find their asses because important stuff was at stake, like determining school districts and funding.

So if the U.S. government admits it undercounts black folks, why wouldn't I think the Nielsen people undercount black and Hispanic and, for that matter, poor white viewers? Come on, now. Let's not be naive about this stuff. The ratings system is flawed in two ways: one, they don't know who's watching, and two, they don't care. As greatly watched as Alex Haley's *Roots* was in 1977, I bet you the audience was a lot greater than we know because of the number of black viewers not even represented. Because of the importance attached to the ratings, because the ratings determine what shows stay on, I think it's in our best interest to challenge the ratings. Good shows that black and white people watch have been canceled, and the reason given was low ratings. But how do we know? We'd have to trust the current ratings system and I just don't.

So, we're not represented in the ratings and we sure aren't represented on the air. How can CBS and NBC have no blacks in lead roles on their shows? I mean, there are almost no blacks on their shows. Thank God for the WB and UPN or we just wouldn't be on television. Some of these shows with all-white casts, I'm wondering if they don't have black friends or coworkers. Damn, real life is more integrated than most of these TV shows. You look at these shows, there's no way of telling that black and Hispanic and Asian people make up more than 25 percent of America. Prime-time network TV in no way reflects the diversity of America, and really doesn't reflect who is watching the most TV. Those are the most underrepresented groups.

And I don't know what's worse, TV or Hollywood.

On the Turner broadcast before the Oscars I had predicted Halle Berry and Denzel Washington would win best actress and best actor. And I was happy not only for the both of them, but for all the black actors and actresses who came before them and had brilliant performances in movies for the past fifty years and never got a sniff of a nomination.

As deserving as Denzel is of that Oscar, I don't

know if he deserved it for *Training Day*. My movie fascination began later in life, when I had time to go to the theater. But I see a whole lot of movies now, and I thought he deserved the Oscar for Best Actor for *The Hurricane* and for *Malcolm X*. It was silly that the problems with the historical accuracy of *The Hurricane* wound up penalizing Denzel. How stupid and how unfair is it to hold *The Hurricane* to this lofty standard when every picture made in Hollywood is dramatized to some extent. All these movies that are "based" on real life or a script or something historic in nature . . . in every one of those damn movies the producer or the screenwriter has taken liberties with the original work. So please don't tell me *The Hurricane* should be treated differently, or that Denzel's portrayal of Hurricane Carter didn't count or needed to be diminished because of it. And Denzel's performance as Malcolm X was one of the great, great performances to me, not just that year but over many years.

As happy as I was that night for Denzel and Halle, I guess the thing that disappointed me the most is that this was, what, the seventy-fifth year of the Academy Awards? After all this time it's a big deal that a black woman and black man win Best Actor and Best Actress? I'll tell you what it is: it's sad. It's sad to be even having this discussion. It's like I said about people making a big deal about Tyrone Willingham being hired as head coach of Notre Dame. If this is a big deal in 2002, we're in trouble. Same goes for black actors winning an Oscar in 2002.

If you don't think prejudice is alive and well, that Oscar night is a damn good reminder. I know there are great white actors and actresses who've never won an Oscar. Bob Hope never won an Oscar. But none of the great black actresses had ever won one, and Sidney Poitier was the only black actor to win one. Then again, it's probably difficult to be considered for the Oscar when all you get to portray is a junkie, a drug dealer, a pimp or a hoodlum. What kind of choices are those? I think Brad Pitt has a few more choices than that, doesn't he? But where are the choices for Morgan Freeman? How come Morgan Freeman gets nominated one year for Best Actor or Best Supporting Actor, then you don't even see his ass for the next two or three years in a meaningful role? How is it that Morgan Freeman and Samuel L. Jackson can be accepted by the moviegoing public one year, then have no choices of reasonable roles the very next year?

Seriously, it's disturbing. The people who go to the movies don't seem to care. They're like sports fans in a way. If word is out that there's a good movie, people are going to want to see it, no matter what color the actor is. Yeah, there are some racists out there who don't want to see blacks or Hispanics or Asians in any mainstream role and don't want their kids to go see those movies. But for the most part, you put good material out there and people are going to go see it. People who go to movies know Morgan Freeman is a great actor. It's the people in Hollywood who don't allow him to have any choice of roles. Man, Hollywood is worse off than sports when it comes to inclusion and diversity. There are no choices, no range of characters for black and Hispanic people.

And just think, Morgan Freeman and Denzel and Halle Berry have it better than just about everybody else. The rest of the brothers better be content to play a drug dealer, a gangsta or a playboy 'cause that's all he's getting to portray. Who is doing the casting for these movies and who holds them accountable? Who's writing the scripts? At least in sports, people know the owner and the general manager and who is doing the hiring, and people can jump on 'em and insist that a league or a sport do better. In sports you tend to know who ought to be accountable. But how many of us know the studio head or an executive producer, and where do you go to make a damn complaint? I'm just so disturbed about this. I had a woman say to me one day last summer, "Charles, you're doing well. . . . I know a lot of black people making money and doing well." And I told her, "Yeah, I do, too. In the NBA." People see a few black celebrities doing well, getting a chance to pursue their ambitions, and they think it's that way across the board. Well, it isn't. If it was, Halle Berry and Denzel winning those Oscars last March wouldn't have been such a huge deal. And neither would Tyrone Willingham being named coach at Notre Dame. But what's going on with the television industry and the movie industry is troubling, especially considering how much the people forgotten by those industries patronize them.

•　　•　　•

My daughter can watch a little bit of television on school nights. But at 9:30, it's going off. When I was growing up, we could watch a couple of hours of TV per night. But my grandmother said the TV was going off at ten, and that was that. But that was a different day: no Turner, no ESPN, no satellite dishes. My grandfather Simon Barkley watched the Atlanta

Braves religiously. He probably watched every game since the Braves moved to Atlanta from Milwaukee in 1966. They were what was on. And the only NFL games we could watch when I was growing up in Alabama involved the Cowboys, the Redskins or the New York Giants. That was it. The affiliates didn't even care about any regional games. (When I became friends with Roy Greene, the thing I used to ride him about, because he played for the Cardinals, was him getting his butt kicked all the time by the Cowboys, Redskins and Giants.) Every Sunday we'd come racing home from church, hoping the NFL game was a 4:00 P.M. game and not a one o'clock game. Same thing in basketball: it was the Celtics, Lakers or 76ers. No local games, no regional games, nothing. And now, you can see it all, whatever you want, twenty-four hours a day. You don't have to worry about what the local affiliate wants to show. You're not at anybody's mercy. It's amazing how you get used to what you have. Now I don't even know how people could live without the dish.

Bobby Knight's Olympics

I was cut by Bobby Knight in the 1984 Olympic Trials. In a way, it was a relief: a big part of me didn't want to make the Olympic basketball team in 1984. Seriously, I didn't. Number one, I didn't like Bobby Knight. And number two, I was leaving Auburn to turn pro. I just went there to help improve my stock for the NBA draft, and I told people as much before I went to Bloomington, Indiana, for the trials. People heard me say that after getting cut from the team and they said, "Oh, you're just saying that because you're disappointed you didn't make the team." But no, that was never the case. When Steve Alford wrote a book—and he was my roommate during the trials—he wrote, "Charles didn't want to make the team."

I didn't want to dedicate my entire summer just to playing basketball. My primary goal was to move up in the draft, which meant working out, getting mentally and physically prepared to play professional basketball. It was about to be my first time leaving Alabama for an extended period. I was leaving school early. What I was about to take on that summer made it a really important time in my life. I wanted to go to the Olympic trials, kick a little butt and move up in the draft. Before the trials, most of the scouts thought I was going to be drafted in the middle of the first round, maybe even late in the first round. But at those trials I got to play against everybody. I mean everybody: Michael Jordan, Patrick Ewing, Chris Mullin, John Stockton, Karl Malone, Sam Perkins, Waymon Tisdale . . . everybody. There are seven, maybe eight guys from those trials going to the Basketball Hall of Fame. Half of the Dream Team was at those trials. I remember coming home after getting cut; John Stockton, Terry Porter and I rode home together. People don't believe this now, but we got cut the same day. That's a lot of NBA experience that got cut that day.

Bobby Knight pretty much just wanted to keep guys he could control. There were a lot of good players who were cut, guys who were better than ones who made the team. Antoine Carr should have made the team. Karl Malone should have made it. I don't think people really remember all the great players who came to those trials. Joe Dumars, A. C. Green, Michael Cage, Dell Curry, Mark Price, Chuck Person, Roy Tarpley. As it turns out, A.C, Joe, Dell, those guys all played in the league more than a dozen years. And those were the guys who got cut. It ain't like those guys went and got good all of a sudden after they left the Olympic trials. Of course they got better, but they were good when they showed up. After the first few obvious guys, Knight kept the guys he could control. There's no doubt in my mind he would have cut me sooner if I hadn't played so well. What people don't remember about the tryouts is that the sessions early in those trials were open to the public and the media. People could see for themselves who could play. It was all out there for everybody to see. We had open scrimmages. I don't care if anybody had heard of John Stockton or not, you knew Stockton could play his ass off. I don't care whether people had heard of Terry Porter or not; the guys on the court knew Porter was one of the best players there. You can't fool the guys on the court. Those guys knew I was one of the top two or three players there. When ESPN interviewed Sam Perkins a couple of years ago for the *Sports-Century* piece on me he said, "When they read the names of the guys who were making the team and I heard Charles didn't make it, I just knew I was getting cut."

And then when we got to the NBA and our careers started to develop immediately, it was obvious Bobby Knight had cut some great players and just kept guys he wanted to keep.

But being able to play with and against those guys was a big turning point for me in my career. That kicked me to a whole different level. You have to remember, just about every great player was at those trials, and you started off being somewhat intimidated. Remember, some of the guys who made the team were Michael, Patrick, Sam Perkins and Chris Mullin. Those guys were on every All-America list. All these guys were there from big-time schools that you'd see on TV all the time but didn't get to play against. But I do remember going home, and when I got back to Alabama my coach said, "What did you think?" And I told him I knew then that if I worked on my game, worked all summer and had myself ready, that I'd be able to play with any player in the country. I knew I'd be able to do well in the NBA because these guys I'd already held my own against at the trials were going to be the stars of the NBA. He'd already told me that. But I had to tell him, "Coach, there was one guy up there who's the best player I've ever seen. It's Michael Jordan. He was the only guy better than me." I've only felt that way twice in my life, that when I was standing there watching a guy, that I knew I was with somebody who was special, who had to be the best at what he did. And the other time was the first time I played golf with Tiger. Those are the only two times I've felt that way. They could just do things athletically and competitively that other people couldn't do.

I don't begrudge Knight anything, nothing at all. I have nothing against him. When he cut me, I thought he felt bad about it. I'd always thought if he cut me he'd be a jerk about it. But he was actually pretty cool.

When that whole thing was over, people asked me, "How come you played so well in the Olympic Trials?" Hell, even though it's always more difficult playing against great players, when you're playing with other great players it ought to be easier. If you're playing with other great players, guys who can all haul their part of the load, all you have to do is play. That's why I feel bad now for Kevin Garnett and Gary Payton in recent years, and for Tim Duncan in the 2001–02 season. They just didn't have enough help. Patrick Ewing, for most of his career, didn't have enough help. As great as they are the game would be so much easier if they had just one other guy. So, the Olympics were easy. I played twice in the Olympics, 1992 and 1996. I led the team both times in scoring and in 1996 in rebounding. I didn't have to do everything, I just had to do my thing. And it was so easy.

A Dream Team

The worst thing about getting cut by Knight in 1984 was that I thought I'd never get the chance to play for another U.S. Olympic team because at that point NBA players weren't eligible. There was no reason to think I'd get another shot. Then, of course, the international demand to see the best basketball players in the world—us—was so overwhelming that the people running the basketball competition made the NBA guys eligible for the 1992 Summer Olympics in Barcelona. That decision, allowing NBA players to compete, changed basketball around the world.

The first real sign of the huge impact the team

would have came when *Sports Illustrated* wanted to put guys on the cover of the magazine. The photo shoot itself was incredible. They got us together at the NBA All-Star Game that February of '92. And it was like the ultimate confirmation. Just standing there with those guys, knowing I was going to play with them, was incredible. You just get chills and you're honored knowing you're going to have the chance to play with players that great.

When people ask me if I have any regrets, I tell them I wish I had gotten to play with an All-Star in his prime for a few years. When I got to Philadelphia, Doc and Moses were older and past their MVP years, and I was very young. And when I got to Phoenix, I had some left, but I was on the downside because I had played eight years in Philly and was starting to have problems with my back. Even though I was voted the league Most Valuable Player my first year in Phoenix, which was the 1992–93 season, I knew I had four seasons better than that in Philly. One year in Philly, I led the league with 14 rebounds a game, and another year I averaged 28 points a game with 11-plus rebounds. Earvin beat me out for MVP honors in one of the closest votes ever at the time. But we didn't contend the way I wanted, the way we all wanted. We never got over trading Brad Daugherty and Moses. We had one real good year with Mike Gminski and Rick Mahorn, 1989–90, when we won 53 games, and finished first in the Atlantic Division ahead of the Celtics and Knicks. But that was the only year we had a really good team. I had more help in Phoenix with Kevin Johnson and Dan Majerle and those guys. But I was in Philly still when the Dream Team was announced in 1991. I was putting up numbers and doing what I felt was the best I could do, but we didn't have great teams then. So being selected to play with the Dream Team was an amazing opportunity. And it let me know what basketball people thought of me and my career. Before the team got together, they picked five to be photographed and be on the cover of *Sports Illustrated*. You're one of the five who represents the country! I figured, "Damn, I guess all my hard work is paying off."

No matter what happens in my life, there will be nothing like that. I've never been with the Beatles but I don't know how they could have been any bigger than us that summer. We had 5,000 people watching us get on the bus every day to go to practice or games. Thousands were lined up on the side of the highway just to see the bus roll by. And they couldn't really see any of us inside. We had two police cars in the front, two police cars in the back, armed guards on both sides of the bus on motorcycles. There were armed guards on the rooftop of the hotel we were staying in. And they moved the front desk of the hotel from the lobby to the very front door. You couldn't enter without picture ID. I loved every day of it, every minute of that summer, that whole experience. How could you not have fun? I'm in the Olympics, a once-in-a-lifetime opportunity.

Here's how unique it was. We were practicing one day when Bishop Desmond Tutu came to the gym. He met with the team, was talking to us, and started crying. He actually told us, "I cannot express to you how much you men mean to people in my country. They love you guys, they know all of you, and you inspire them."

Ten years have passed now and some kids are too young to remember, and some folks have forgotten, but at the time we were certainly an international example of proof that black people can do great things. When Bishop Tutu said how much we meant to young people in South Africa, he had tears in his eyes and my heart was racing. I'm like, "Damn, I inspire somebody in South Africa? Bishop Desmond Tutu is telling me I inspire somebody, that I'm affecting people's lives, that I'm large in South Africa?" It was completely unbelievable. He said, "Please keep up the good work because most of these kids know nothing but heartache." I'm thinking, "Holy shit!" He brought with him ten, twelve kids who all had our jerseys on. It was very, very inspiring. It's one of those episodes in life you think back on and it seems like a dream. But even with that kind of attention, guys didn't walk around acting full of themselves. I think we were more grateful than anything to be part of something so unique and so important to the sports world. Even though this was the greatest collection of players ever assembled on one team, we never had any ego problems. That didn't mean it wasn't as competitive as hell. In fact, it was the most competitive thing you ever wanted to see.

Clyde Drexler, who was still with Portland at the time, wanted to prove he was as good as Michael Jordan, which nobody was. And Michael just wanted to torch Clyde, so Clyde and Michael went at each other. Scottie Pippen wanted to guard Magic all the time, which was a great, great matchup. This was a year after the Bulls had beaten the Lakers in the NBA Finals, and Magic wanted to go back after Scottie. You had David Robinson going against Patrick Ewing in a classic big man matchup. Karl Malone and I were trying to prove who was the best power forward in the world so we were going at each other every day.

The practices were just damn war. Obviously, we've all got egos, and we're all competitive, so that made it as intense as it could possibly be. And Chuck Daly just sat back and said, "Wow!" It was just phenomenal. Chuck had two complete units. There were twelve on the roster, so one guy each day just had to check his ego, plus Christian Laettner, but we didn't give a shit about his playing time because he was the one college player on the team. People have to remember how successful a career Christian had at Duke. It had to be difficult for any college player, even one who had won two NCAA championships, to come in and try to play with that group. We rode him a little bit, but it was good, harmless posturing. I like Christian because he handled it so well. Some people go back and forth about who should have had that last spot on the team. I don't know and I don't care. It's like the All-Star Game and being voted MVP. A lot of guys have All-Star-caliber seasons, but don't make the team. Shaq, like Michael Jordan used to be, is always the MVP, but doesn't always get voted the award. A lot of people say Isiah Thomas should have been on the Dream Team. But the one NBA player who never got the credit I think he deserves was Dominique Wilkins. It's very much like the naming of the Fifty Greatest NBA Players. I thought that Connie Hawkins should have made it. I thought Bob McAdoo should have made it. I thought Joe Dumars could have made it. Somebody is going to be left out and there are going to be hard feelings. But once that group was together we enjoyed each other and the experience, and we also realized the historical significance.

By 1996, when the Summer Olympics were in Atlanta, we had guys bitching about playing time, guys who made life miserable. It was so frustrating. There were two games where I just said to Lenny Wilkens, who was the head coach of that team, "Coach, don't play me tonight. I don't want these guys bitching about playing time." By 1996, you could also see the other countries really coming up. The only real advantage we had now, and it was only four years later, was depth. In 1992 those teams could put three or four quality NBA players out on the floor, but no more than that. And we won those games by an average margin of 44 points in Barcelona. Even the best European teams would have to bring some young upstart who wasn't ready off the bench. By 1996, they were putting five, sometimes six quality players out there. And the average margin of victory was down to something like 30 points per game. And you could see certain European teams catching up with us in depth and athleticism. And you know we could have, probably should have lost that game to Croatia in 2000 in Sydney. Now, we may not lose a game in the next Olympics in Athens in 2004, but we could lose a game and really struggle in 2008. The only way the teams around the world had any chance of getting better was to play against us in international competition. And they knew that, and they were willing to take their lumps at the beginning.

In '92, the games were easy, but there was stress because we didn't realize when the competition first started that we were that much better than everybody else. We'd never played against those guys before. We knew we had better not lose, so we were on guard. Once the game started, we realized those guys couldn't beat us, but we still wanted everybody to know Americans were the best in the world at basketball so we gave it everything we had.

But with all that competitiveness going on, even with guys trying to beat each other's brains out in practice, for the most part we put it aside at night. Larry Bird and Patrick Ewing became great friends, and we called 'em Larry and Harry. That's the great thing about sports. You make friendships that people never could have predicted and half the damn time they don't understand how it happened. Me, Scottie, Michael and Magic played cards every night, all night. We'd start playing cards around eight o'clock, go until five in the morning, get three hours' sleep and then go to practice. Every day. Every single day. And I'm not talking about just in Barcelona, or even Monte Carlo, but starting back when we started practicing and having those exhibition games all around the country. I can remember the Tournament of the Americas, staying up all night every night.

One night though, and I'll never forget this, we had the most uncomfortable moment. But it also tells you how much respect I have for Earvin Johnson. Remember, Earvin had announced he was HIV-positive in November of 1991, which just stunned us all.

We're playing cards late one night, watching HBO in whoever's hotel room it was. And a comedian starts crackin' on Earvin, saying, "Can you believe that Magic Johnson has the AIDS virus? Man got all that damn money and too cheap to spend $2 to buy a box of condoms." The guy was pretty funny and you wanted to laugh, but you couldn't because you're sitting in the room with the guy he's cracking on, and he's your close friend and your teammate, and just the greatest guy in the world. The comedian goes on and on and says more funny stuff. And it's just so uncomfortable. Finally, Earvin says, "Man, that's some funny shit, isn't it? You guys go ahead and laugh." And we were all like, "Whew!" It's something that we had never talked about that summer; you can't bring it up. It's just so difficult to talk about. But at that moment I thought, "This is going to be uncomfortable sometimes, but it really could be all right."

Every Minute of Every Day Cannot Be Serious

Not long ago, I was in Australia and somebody for some reason had a tableful of rubies, between $750,000 and $1 million of rubies just sitting on a table. And I said, "Damn, must not be any black folks in Australia. You can't just leave $1 million worth of jewelry lying around in the 'hood." And of course, somebody got mad and pretty soon the NAACP was calling me, upset and angry about what I'd said. I told whoever called me, "Man, I'm silly like that sometimes. Every minute of every day cannot be serious because you'd go crazy." I'll say to white folks at a party, "Man, there's nothing in the world that makes me as nervous as seeing white people dance."

I'm going to have fun with everybody. Anybody who knows me also knows that nobody is spared. You can never make the case that I'm picking on one group. You've got to lighten the mood sometimes, whether we're talking in the locker room before a big, important game, or whether we're talking about some real-life issue. Humor should make people feel a little better.

Shannon Sharpe, the NFL tight end, and I are similar in a lot of ways. We both try to do it with humor. Everybody's sense of humor isn't the same, we know that. But if you don't try to deal with sensitive shit by making it funny, they're going to call you militant. I'm thinking, "I'm trying to put some stuff out there to get us talking." But you better make it funny or some people just won't be able to stand it. It goes down better with a little humor, and people tend to see that even though you've got these concerns, you're still a human being and you can share a laugh.

Of course, it's gotten me in trouble. There was the night during a Turner broadcast, at the time when the PETA people were in the process of forcing the NBA and NCAA to use synthetic basketballs instead of leather, that I said that the only thing animals were good for was eating and wearing.

Another time I said to a white reporter I know, "I hate white folks." I was talking to a writer I'd known for years and years. And I asked him later if he had taken offense, and I believe he wrote a piece in his newspaper that said he was never offended. He was actually offended that somebody who wasn't involved in the conversation in the first place had come in and interpreted something without knowing the relationship between me and the reporter. So where's the context? If you just put that on the air and you don't know the relationship of the two people, what was being discussed, what the mood was, are you informing the viewer of anything or just inflaming?

If you know the people involved, can you not tell an off-color joke anymore? Are we that screwed up? The media has us so screwed up right now that we think every sentence that comes out of everybody's mouth has to be politically correct. That's bullshit. I tell you what; if the politically correct police ever came into a professional locker room . . . oh my God . . . we could start World War III every day in there. I wish I was on a team right now with a bunch of Catholic guys, with everything that's gone on recently in the Catholic Church. Damn, I'd be killing them guys, just killing them. And, of course, I know there's a very serious element to the charges of sexual abuse. The priests guilty of sexually abusing those kids–they're minors–ought to be put in jail as far as I'm concerned, as I've said. It's a serious story. But don't tell me that's going to be off-limits in a locker room, because it isn't. If I was playing with my man Joe Kleine, who is Catholic, right now, oh, he would never catch a break.

Thank God for Jerry Springer's show. I thought only black folks were that screwed up until I watched Jerry Springer. The beauty of that show, of all those daytime shows, is that they show how screwed up everybody is, regardless of race, ethnic background, gender or anything else. If you can sit back and get a good laugh from that stuff . . .

But one of the reasons I need to be really careful about what I say on television is that I know people are going to believe it and take everything so literally. And you know how I like to joke and have fun and poke fun at certain things or institutions. But somebody sitting out there in South Dakota who has a different sense of humor may say, "That guy is an asshole." That's why on the basketball show, I'll try to stay away from personality a whole lot, especially when I'm being critical. Now, I'm going to take on things I think are wrong or people in big places. But I have to remind myself about how people are going to take things.

But I still think we need to be able to poke fun at one another. I told somebody not too long ago who is short that little people shouldn't be riding in first class during flights. Little people should ride in coach. You know if you're little. I don't fly first class because I need better meals. I do it because of size. I hate when you walk through first class and you've got little two-foot people filling up the first class seats while all the tall people are walking to the back of the plane. It's about comfort. Those two-foot people can be comfortable in coach. If you're 6-2 you can't even get your damn knees inside the seat in front of you. I don't know how anybody taller than 6-4 can sit in those seats. And the airline executives don't give a damn 'cause they never walk back there in the first place. I don't fly first class because I've got a lot of money. I do it because I need the room. But sometimes, it's not available, so I have to sit in coach, next to a person who's going to talk my ear off and ask me, "How did it feel to play against Michael Jordan?"

Young Players Don't Get It

People ask me all the time, if I was coming out of high school today and was a great player, would I even go to college? And the answer is yes, I would go to college.

Realistically, none of these guys are ready for the NBA the first couple of years they come out, not professionally and not personally. The best-possible-case scenarios were Kevin Garnett, Kobe Bryant and Tracy McGrady, and it still took them three years to become real NBA players. Jermaine O'Neal is a nice kid and a nice player but he's not The Man yet, and it took him four years plus, and the team that initially invested all that money and time and tutoring in him didn't even get to reap the benefits. The Toronto Raptors invested everything in McGrady, and he's in Orlando now. So what kind of sense did that make from a competitive standpoint? You're not only counting on that guy panning out, but still being with your team when he pans out.

Then there are the guys who get drafted out of high school and don't make it, like Korleone Young and Leon Smith. And they have no eligibility left to start in college, where they should have started in the first place. Guys now just can't wait to get to the pros, or even spend the time to make themselves really good players, which is really the best way to guarantee you get paid the maximum amount of money.

It all starts very early now. When I was young, we didn't have AAU teams. Now, these kids are playing in AAU leagues and they're in competitive situations all the time. They travel and play on the road. They've got adults telling them how great they are all the time. We weren't getting attention and praise and, in some cases, money from AAU coaches. We didn't have shoe companies giving us shoes. We didn't have none of that stuff. So they're just spoiled rotten from the very beginning. Most of them don't even know that fifteen years ago NBA teams flew commercial.

But the problem is very, very complex because most of the kids who do go to college aren't getting what they've been promised. There is no significant graduation rate among Division I college athletes anymore, at least not in men's basketball. Didn't I just hear during the 2002 NCAA men's basketball tournament that something like twenty-four or twenty-five out of the sixty-five schools in the field hadn't graduated a single player within the last five years? That's ridiculous. What graduation rate? Not giving money—at least a stipend—to these kids who produce all this revenue is a scam anyway. That's what I've always thought. CBS just paid more than $6 billion for the right to televise the games. Who do we think made the tournament worth that much money? Those kids who play made it worth that much. That's why the NCAA and the networks, and whoever is involved with putting on these games and making all that money, need to figure out a way to give them at least a stipend.

Now, the good old boys used to take the position that these kids were getting tuition, room and board and a good education. But if you look at these graduation percentages, low as they are, you can't even take the position that they're getting an education anymore. They're not graduating. They're not graduating at all, and the ones who don't make the pros—which is most of them—are screwed. We're sending a bunch of dummies out into the real world with no education, with no real way to make themselves attractive candidates for employment, and they're screwed. That's all they are. The biggest schools seem like they're graduating about 10 percent of their players, so this whole thing needs to be reevaluated.

Those kids who go to big schools to play sports but are only reading at fourth- and fifth-grade levels shouldn't be in Division I colleges in the first place. The recruiters and the admissions people knew every one of their test scores and their GPAs and reading levels before they recruited them. Seriously, how fair is this to the kid? This kid is struggling to make it in high school and he's going to do college course work and play Division I sports at the same time? And he's going to do it for nothing, in a lot of cases while his family has zero money? All this because he can help put 100,000 fans in the stands on Saturday afternoon?

A whole lot of these kids who are turning professional out of high school should go to some form of minor leagues. Every NBA team should have multiple affiliated minor league teams. These kids aren't ready when they come out of high school, but most of 'em also aren't interested in going to college. And anybody who tells you these kids get better sitting on the bench in the pros than they do playing in college, they're lying. You're not getting better sitting on the bench.

The reason I want to see the pros make better use of a minor league or this new developmental league the NBA started, or whatever you want to make available, is that it just isn't fair, it ain't moral, to just use a kid to make millions of dollars for a school and just turn him loose on the world uneducated with no chance to succeed. If you bring a kid into school you know has little chance to graduate just to help you make money by appearing on television and helping you fill your stands every week, and then say after four years, "See ya!," well, what the hell is that?

I know that not every kid who goes to college is interested in an education. A whole lot of 'em are trying to get to the NBA or NFL and that's their only goal. But the entire big-time college athletic system encourages this stuff.

My first day at Auburn—and I'm presuming this happens at a whole lot of other schools, too—they asked, "Do you want to stay eligible or do you want to graduate?" Hell, you're eighteen years old and you don't want to flunk out of college after one year so you say, "Yeah, I want to be eligible." I'm just tired of hearing that if you go to these schools you're getting something, that you're getting a college education. You're not getting a college education if the graduation rates are what we're being told.

And what makes it really bad is they're not graduating and they're not making themselves great basketball players either. But they come into the pros and think they are. Young guys now aren't nearly as accepting of criticism from coaches as we were. I'm talking about even the mildest criticism. They're not even receptive to their parents' criticism. Basic coaching is something they consider criticism. I guess it's like that for kids of this era no matter what they do. I have friends in the media who tell me the same thing about young reporters. But society has done this. Mainstream society has made every single thing about money. Basketball, football, network TV, it's all the same. When I look at a show like *Fear Factor*, what the hell is that but some quickie, gimmicky way to make money? And a network will put that on, which encourages young writers to turn out a piece of junk 'cause they'll make some money right away, instead of putting on quality programming. That would reinforce the idea of working harder to develop something of higher quality. People don't want to work to develop skills if they see some quickie, gimmick way to make money. All these reality shows on TV now, that's all they are about, instant money and instant notoriety and becoming some celebrity wannabe.

I know I sound like an older guy now just attacking young guys, and I know it sounds like jealousy. But damn, we're right. The older guys are right in this case. In terms of basketball, the game is not the same. It's entirely money-driven. It was always like that for the owners and networks and sponsors. But it's become like that for the players, too. The owners have always been greedy, but the players have turned into the same people as the owners, and that's amazing to me.

To me, the whole process just screws the fans. You know if you draft a high school player he isn't going to help your team for three years. Kobe Bryant, great as he is, didn't help the Lakers until his third year. But that's not the way drafts are designed in any sport. The purpose of a draft is for the worst teams in that sport to get immediate relief from losing by drafting the best player available. The worst teams draft first for one damn reason: immediate help. What the hell is immediate about waiting three years on a high school guy to develop and mature? When you do that you're telling your fans publicly, "Hey, we're getting better. We just need you to keep paying $75 a game for those season tickets for the next three years. We're going to make money, we're going to be bad in the meantime, and that's just the way it is. Just hold on." What a scam. It's just not right.

The owners say they don't want it. They say that they prefer not having these high school kids and the guys who play maybe one year in college in the draft. But most owners do want it. Why? Because it's an effective way to keep salaries down long term. Teams can let some high-priced veteran go, but keep a kid who for three years is making chump change comparatively because of the current collective bargaining agreement that has predetermined his salary. And in most cases, that kid can't become a good enough player sitting on the bench to make the maximum after three years. As good as Jermaine O'Neal is now, he's an excellent example of what I'm talking about. He wasn't good enough after his first contract to sign for the maximum because he'd been sitting on the bench in Portland for four years. So he signs a contract, he's tied up in his second contract for six or seven years, making money based on what he had shown in Portland, which wasn't much. So now he's behind the earning curve. For some guys, that translates into making $5 million a year instead of $9 million or $11 million, which is why I believe despite what they say a lot of owners are in favor of letting these high school kids come into the league. They're saving money. That's how you make it so fewer guys will make the maximum amounts allowed by the bargaining agreement.

It's not like every owner is making all his decisions based on trying to win a championship. I'm serious about this; there are only about five or six teams that are seriously trying to win a championship every year. The rest of 'em keep recycling young guys they get in the lottery every year, then they keep letting 'em go just when they become eligible for big contracts. The Clippers are the best example of that in the NBA. They've perfected it. They get these guys relatively cheap in the draft, take all that season ticket money while the guys are young and developing, then when it's time to pay these guys and put a decent team on the floor, the Clippers let 'em go. Just look at the players they've gotten rid of just when those guys have gotten to be good players, as far back as World B. Free, Tom Chambers and Terry Cummings. Every time it's time for them to pay somebody big money and really start to build a team, they let him go. They get back in the lottery, get some new hope through the draft, and the fans don't know, they're getting all excited. Let's see what the Clippers do now. They've got a chance to pay Elton Brand, Lamar Odom and Michael Olowo-kandi. Two of them, I believe, will wind up being let go by the Clippers.

I think players always underestimate how smart and how savvy the owners are about money and about business in general. They're megamillionaires for a reason. When we had those meetings before the management lockout of labor in 1999, which led the league to cancel half the season, I said, "Hey guys, we're going to lose. Those guys are billionaires. We're millionaires. They're smarter than we are on mone-tary issues." I told 'em, "We're gonna have guys killing themselves before they can outlast the owners." And there we were a few weeks later, could have had the same deal we wound up taking without losing three months' pay. Hell, we probably could have gotten that deal two years earlier.

People have been made to think these owners have to win to make money, that all they're concerned about is winning. Don't believe that. They're making money without winning, which is why they're not selling these teams. These guys didn't get to be as rich as they are by being stupid. If they weren't making money, they wouldn't be in the business. And in the process, the fans get screwed because you know when you draft a high school player he's not going to help your team for three years–if at all.

People will say that I'm against the young boys, but it's just the opposite. We older guys want these young boys to do well. But they don't look at the situation critically. Becoming a free agent before you have a chance to become as good a player as you can be doesn't help you make more money. In some cases it limits what you can make.

But guys think if we offer advice or try to get them to see the big picture that we're against them. There's definitely a large generation gap right now. My last couple of years in the league I was trying to work with Steve Francis. I was trying to teach him some of the right ways to do certain things, and while I think he understood what I was trying to do in the end, it was a struggle the whole way. For the longest time, he didn't look at me as a player who'd already experienced life in the NBA trying to help him. I think he looked at me as an old guy criticizing him while trying to still be The Man.

There are things I just think young players don't need, and probably hurt them professionally and financially. For example, I'm trying to figure out how entourages, which you only used to see in boxing, became such a big part of pro basketball. Nobody ever in the old days had an entourage. This is all new crap, New Jack stuff. I'm still trying to figure out what you need them for. Guys have drivers and all this crap. They're essentially just guys on payroll, draining your money. Is there a white player in professional sports with an entourage? I don't think so.

If somebody in your entourage does something stupid or negative, it's the player who's going to get the blame because he's the guy in the public eye. He's the guy whose name everybody knows and the guy with everything at stake. I've never had an entourage, but it seems to me it's just a bunch of people hanging around, spending your money, putting you in jeopardy. What's the point of that?

When I was young, I had older guys on their way out take me aside and offer advice. Some of it might have been critical, but I listened because it was obvious to me they had been there and done that and they had my best interests at heart. It's the same now, we older guys have the interests of the young guys at heart when we make a critical observation. But they don't see it that way and we all wish they would.

God Doesn't Have a Favorite Team

Athletic competition is emotional enough without bringing religion into it. More wars have been fought over religious conflict than anything else, so clearly it's an explosive issue.

I don't think religion and sports should mix. There are so many different religions, and for the most part we only understand our own. People might want to be tolerant of views different from their own, but from what I've observed we don't understand other people's religions. Even a lot of smart people who deal with complex things in their lives every day can't understand the rituals or the philosophies of other religions. And that ignorance often just opens up a huge box of problems and issues.

Look at professional sports nowadays. A team is a lot like most other workplaces, just smaller. People are from every part of the globe, speaking a hundred different languages and practicing a hundred different religions. And most of the time we haven't even been exposed to even half the religions being practiced by guys who are our teammates or the guys we're playing against. So how can you have a couple of guys who may be practicing one form of religion dictating to the whole team, telling a team full of guys practicing different religions to do one thing? Look at any NBA team. It's very possible you can have Protestants, Catholics, Muslims and atheists represented on one team. And now guys are coming in from China and bringing their religions with them. You're not going to get everybody to agree on anything. You're not going to get a consensus as it relates to religion.

And it's just wrong, in my opinion, to act as if your religion is more important than somebody else's. Just because one player is outnumbered doesn't mean his religion is less important. That would cause resentment and all kinds of problems within a team.

And that's not even the biggest problem with religion in sports in my opinion. You know what else bothers me about religion in sports? God doesn't have a favorite team. I don't like to hear guys after they win a match or a game or a fight go into an interview and say, "God was on my side." How stupid is it to presume that God has a favorite team, or that he would take your side against your opponent? Where did that stuff come from? How religious are you really if you think God doesn't care about the guy on the other side of the field, or the other side of the court, or in the other corner?

I just don't think it's fair that people assume they can determine the actions of others because of religion. Kevin Johnson, my teammate in Phoenix, is really religious. And before one of the Game 7s of a playoff series we played during my time with the Suns he and a couple of other guys talked the whole team into going to a prayer meeting. And I told them, "No, I'm not going." I said, "Number one, God doesn't have a favorite team. And number two, doesn't it seem like we're praying to God to win us a game when he must have more important things to worry about than this basketball game?" I hope and I pray God has more important things on his mind than some game. I can't believe with all the serious stuff going on today in the world–terrorism, war, hunger, poverty, violence, hatred–that guys think their football or basketball game that day is the most important thing God might have to deal with.

It's not like religion isn't part of my life, because it is. I grew up going to church. I believe in prayer and treating people the way you would want to be treated. But the idea that God might help me beat another team never crossed my mind.

How come it's often the most religious people who seem to forget the verse in the Bible which says that only God can judge men? I was reading something Lee Trevino said, that unless you're a minister, preacher or rabbi you should never be pushing your religious beliefs on people. That's pretty much the way I feel. Religion, to me, is your individual relationship with God, or whatever you call your Supreme Being. That's it, plain and simple. My belief is that there is a Supreme Being. I don't get into whether he's black, white, man or woman.

I do think that God, by whatever name you want to use, gave me a special gift. One of my close friends who is an agnostic said to me, "Why do you thank God when you play well?" And I said, "I'm really thanking him for allowing me to be healthy and for giving me this gift, not that I played well in a specific game." He said, "Then how is it that when something bad happens you never acknowledge God?" That really made me think. I said, "That's fair. I don't know the answer, but that's fair."

I'm just not going to walk around and talk about God all the time like a lot of players. I don't think that proves to anybody how religious you are. A whole lot of people never talk openly about their religion; you don't even know what, if any, religion or God they believe in. But they treat people the way they would like folks to treat them.

I know a lot of people don't want to accept that, or they want organized religion to be more involved in everything. But to me, religion opens up the biggest can of worms, and I just try to keep it away from sports because the bottom line is, God doesn't have a favorite team.

My Dad

My dad made me feel horrible when I didn't graduate from high school. I had flunked my final exam in Spanish and couldn't graduate until after I passed it in summer school. He flew all the way across the country to see me graduate, and when he couldn't, he took his disappointment out on me. He screamed, "I can't believe I flew all the way from California, that I came all the way across the damn country to see this ceremony and you aren't even going to graduate."

I never did march. It was my fault I flunked Spanish, and it took me a long time to get over that. I had to take it again in summer school. It taught me that you aren't going to be given anything in life, that you have to earn what you get. It was my life and my fault. And I feel bad I blamed it on other people. But my dad wasn't concerned with that important lesson, just that he was inconvenienced. It turned out that he motivated me the first few years—unintentionally—because I was so angry at him. For the longest time I tried, then for years I just didn't talk to him. I was angry and it was too frustrating. I'm positive my old man never saw me play a basketball game in high school, never saw me play at Auburn. He never saw me play until I got in the NBA. He got interested in a relationship again when I became an NBA All-Star. He was living out in Los Angeles, and he always wanted me to visit him when we played out there. So finally, I started to visit him, spend some time with him when I went out there. But it seemed every time I went to L.A. all of our time was spent with him introducing me to all of his friends, his coworkers and associates. And it was clear what was going on there; he was just showing me off. I was his show pony.

It would make me so damn angry. I mean, I felt this way for years. And finally I had to get to the point where I realized that he had his own life. He had a totally separate existence in which I didn't even matter to him. He wasn't walking around all pissed off; I was. This shit was on my mind all the time, but not his.

But one time a few years ago he became sick for a while and I began thinking, "I've only got one father." And as a result, I'm trying now. I'm making a real effort to extend myself, to get to know him better and let him get to know me better. But I did tell him, "Don't try to be a dad now; it's too late for that. Let's be cordial. Let's be friends." You can't be father-son this late in the game when you haven't actually had that relationship all your life.

At this point in my life I just want to be at peace with my dad. You get one dad, so there's no sense in being pissed off about what happened, whatever void you might have felt in your life. He's not going to live forever, and I don't want to look back and feel I squandered the time. I want him to know his granddaughter. One of the positive things that come from this is I know my relationship with my father–or lack thereof–affects my feeling about fatherhood, about participating and not just being there to take the bows. At the same time, he cannot be my dad, he can only be my friend.

September 11

Normally when I travel from my home in Phoenix to Atlanta to work for TBS and TNT, I catch the midnight red-eye flight to Atlanta. I hop on that flight, get served a late meal, then go to sleep before landing in Atlanta at 6:00 A.M. or whatever it is. That's what used to happen before September 11, 2001. And of course, everything changed for everybody in different ways. For people who travel for a living, the change was dramatic and damn sure immediate. For the first six to eight weeks after September 11, I flew private jets to Atlanta. I couldn't bring myself to fly commercial. After a while I flew commercial again, but now I don't sleep. I'm exhausted, but I can't sleep. I know I'm not alone in having this experience. It's two in the morning and I can't sleep on a flight I used to sleep on all the time because now I'm looking over my shoulder for al Qaeda.

People who don't travel might not understand. People who do travel frequently probably understand completely. I don't sleep because I'm thinking, "You need a chance to fight if somebody makes a move toward that cockpit and you can't give yourself a chance to fight if you're sound asleep." So you don't sleep. You can't sleep. I know if I see or hear somebody running down the aisle toward that cockpit, I'm going to be trying to kick his ass. When I'm flying now I'm sweating and nervous. This is all new for me because I was never a nervous flier. I could fall asleep in a heartbeat. But I can't anymore. This is the world in which we live now. It's a world where you can't let your guard down. You can't let your kids play outside alone anymore without adult supervision. You can't really let any kid out of your sight. And it's like this because there are some profoundly evil people in the world now. It has nothing to do with race or ethnicity. There are just evil people whose primary objectives are to destroy, and so now we're in this place in our history where we have to be on guard and sometimes there's just no place for falling asleep.

On Tuesday, September 11, I was at home in Philly, just getting up to get ready to get on the Metroliner to go to New York City for Joe Pesci's charity golf tournament. My secretary called and said, "What are you doing? Well, you're not going to New York today. You'd better turn on the television."

When I turned on the TV neither tower had fallen yet. But both towers had been attacked. I just sat there the whole day in a trance. I watched it all day, every moment. Six or eight hours later I went out to get something to eat, and then I went right back to watching it. I guess my primary emotion was sadness. It's just so sad to me that there's this kind of evil on the planet, people this evil among human beings. And it's not just the terrorist acts against the United States, it's the kidnapping and killing of young kids, the shootings in these schools. I'm just nervous and sad that there are so many bad people in the world. I guess I was in shock, just numb over the whole thing.

The thing I'll admit to hoping for in the wake of 9/11 was a kinder and gentler America. And I'm sure there are people out there who were so profoundly affected that they changed some basic things about their lives, like the way they treat people, the way they conduct themselves professionally or personally. I figured—and I guess I was really naive—that as horrible and as tragic as this was, it was a chance for people to pull together and fundamentally change things about ourselves and about our country. How could you not hope that when you're watching policemen and firemen and average citizens risk their lives to help people? The way people came to each other's rescue, you had to be inspired and hopeful something productive could eventually come from this. I know I was. I thought, "Okay, we've got a chance now to be better to each other and just be more respectful of each other." People were on TV saying this would change us forever. How could you watch what happened in the days immediately after 9/11 and not feel "We're all in this together"?

You know how long things were different?

It didn't even last two full weeks. Four days? Maybe a week. That's about it. Maybe it was longer in New York because of the impact there, but that's it. But everywhere else, it was business as usual. Democrat vs. Republican, liberal vs. conservative, black vs. white. We didn't even get to October and we were pitted against each other again. Damn. I have to admit I was disappointed because I figure we all want the same things out of life. People, regardless of what race or ethnic group, seem to want to join in the pursuit of happiness, personally and professionally. But if that tragedy and the response to it can't rally us for more than a week, then what the hell can? In a week's time we were back to the same old life of lying and stealing and cheating poor folks and killing children. If we're going to fight off all this evil, we've got to do better. We've got to pull together.

Moses Was Right

I modeled my game after Adrian Dantley and John Drew because they were undersized guys who had to play inside offensively but also had some perimeter skills they developed over the years that helped them evolve and become complete players. Dantley's 6-5, if that tall, and he averaged 25 points for fifteen years and 6 or 7 rebounds a game early in his career. Drew was 6-6, if that, and he averaged 20 points a game and was a 10-rebound-per-game guy when he was young. So at just under 6-5, I really studied those guys and what they did.

I had a coach at Auburn, Roger Banks. He was

Sonny Smith's assistant when I was in college. And because he had coached John Drew at Gardner-Webb, I got to meet Drew and be like a little brother. And we'd talk about basketball and life. He was giving me a ride once in his car–I'm talking about a $75,000 Mercedes–and he said to me, "Son, I snorted up about twenty of these. I've messed up so much money. I've got kids all over the place." He told me, "Look, I'll work with you on your game, but if you're going to listen to anything I say, listen to me when I tell you not to do drugs." I'm sitting there thinking, "Damn." He told me about one Friday night when he got a big pile of coke, got naked, and snorted it all up, and didn't wake up until Saturday just in time to make the game. I was a freshman or sophomore at Auburn when I heard this story. And it had an unbelievable effect on me.

But after a while, I didn't see John again, and I mean for years and years. I just didn't know where he was. His last year in the league was 1984–85, which was my rookie year. He was only thirty years old that season but he played in just nineteen games for Utah. And then it was like he just disappeared.

Anyway, I was still playing in Philly–I don't remember the exact year but I was with the 76ers through the 1992 season—and we were on the road in Houston one night, we were right in front of the hotel at the Galleria. And this homeless guy walks right up to me and grabs me. I mean, the guy is just a bum, dirty and shabby. And he's a big guy and he's really on me, so I rear back to knock the shit out of him. But first I look. It's John Drew. I was in total shock. I mean, I don't even know what I said to him. Here's a man who was a two-time NBA All-Star, a guy who had a productive eleven-year career who must have come in contact with all kinds of people, and he was homeless, a bum on the streets. I gave him all the money I had in my pocket, which must have been several hundred dollars, maybe $500. And then I went up to my hotel room and cried. I couldn't get over it then, and I still can't get over it. And I haven't seen him since, don't know where he is, can't find him. I don't know anybody who knows where he is. It just shocked me so bad. Even though you know somebody's life can go bad when he's on drugs, you don't think it can go that bad. And I keep thinking back to when I was in college, him virtually begging me not to do drugs and not do the kind of stuff that would throw my life off course.

Man, you can find physically talented guys anywhere. It's as if they grow on trees. A whole lot of people have talent. And so many of them don't know how to use it, or they put themselves in positions where they sabotage their own careers. I was thinking about doing another book, a where-are-they-now type book on all the guys I've been with and around, who played from high school to the pros. I really wonder where they all are now. Just 'cause a guy has talent doesn't mean he's going to make it. We assume guys are going to "get it" and they don't. J. R. Rider is an example of a really talented guy, smart guy, too, who never got it. Richard Dumas was way, way up there in terms of talent. Oliver Miller. Kenny Green from Wake Forest. One day a week, Kenny Green was the best player in the world in practice. He was so scary-good you'd say to yourself, "If this guy ever gets it, he'll be dangerous." But they don't get it. They're too immature or too something to ever "get it."

When I first got to Philadelphia in the summer of 1984, Moses Malone told me, "You can come in here every day and work your ass off and still not make it. But I can guarantee you if you come in here and don't work you won't make it." The second thing he told me was, "There are going to be big decisions you'll have to make and you don't have the luxury of making them in private. One mistake can hurt you. If you put yourself in positions where you're vulnerable, it's on you. Use your head."

The physical talent, everybody who makes it to a certain point has that. Then what? Guys screw it up, that's what. Jayson Williams is a perfect example. He signed that contract with the Nets for $100 million, and even though he got hurt and had to retire earlier than he wanted, he still had the world in his hand one minute. On national TV, making a second career for himself. The next minute it's all gone. He's facing jail time and the money he made could be gone in a civil suit. I know Jayson and he's a good guy and I just feel bad, but that's such an example of one mistake. We could sit here and talk about basketball stuff, but it's the management of your life that is really the big difference between making it and not making it for a lot of guys, or hanging on versus making it big. If you don't start with that, you're wasting your time. I've probably played with twenty players who should have played in the NBA for a long time but didn't. It's because their heads weren't together. You see guys with talent all the time who can't make it.

And leaders are even harder to find in sports because most guys want to do it by example, when there's more responsibility involved than that. It's difficult to do because you can't worry about what others think or say. You can't put your efforts into pleasing folks. I had Julius Erving and Moses Malone as leaders, so I got to play with two great ones. It's not a coincidence that in their prime they were able to lead a team to a championship, and Doc was able to lead them to the Finals three other times.

You have to be obsessed to get to the NBA Finals, and I'm not talking about just one guy or just the best player on the team, but everybody. That first year in Phoenix that we reached the Finals, nobody cared about contracts or the number of minutes he played or the number of shots he got or who had the most endorsements. But what you see often in team sports is that after you win once or get to the championship series, guys start saying, "I need more minutes than him," or "I should be making more money than that guy," and when that's the case, you ain't gonna win. That's what happened to us in Phoenix after that first season.

But one guy who really helped me while I was in Phoenix was Paul Silas, who was an assistant under Paul Westphal. Paul Silas helped me with how to judge whether a guy could play, who could play and who couldn't. My fourth and final season in Phoenix, which was 1995–96, I thought we had a really good team. Paul said, "Nope, we really don't have that good a team." And he was right. I'm not surprised by Paul's success as a head coach one bit. Really, he should have gotten a job a lot sooner. Way too much time passed and far too many guys were hired between the time Paul got fired from the Clippers in 1983 and hired again, by Charlotte, in 1998. Hell, the Clippers were still playing in San Diego in 1983. There were something like 140 coaches hired between the time he was fired from his first job and hired in Charlotte.

I've been fortunate to play for several different guys who were good leaders, good coaches, good communicators. Paul Westphal, who I played for in Phoenix, is a great person. No better person ever coached in the NBA, I can say that with certainty. Billy Cunningham was a strict disciplinarian, and he was a great coach for me as a rookie because he provided a lot of structure and discipline. Rudy T. is a great coach for a veteran team because he's more lax. There are a lot of people who have very different personalities who can lead teams effectively in their own ways. Same thing goes for certain players. Mark West, who I played with in Phoenix, is a guy who you'll never hear mentioned as a great leader. But he was a great guy and knew the subtleties of the game and could communicate with the star players or the role players. I had started to develop Michael's mentality, hollering and screaming at guys and beating the hell out of my team. But we had Oliver Miller and Richard Dumas, guys you couldn't scream at and get any results because they were too immature. Mark came to me and said, "Listen, man, you can't put the hammer down on these guys every day, you've got to take a different approach with them."

You see how Bill Cartwright has done a nice job with the Bulls? I know it's early and he's got a long way to go with a young team. But we really shouldn't be that surprised because Bill had more influence with those championship Bulls teams than people thought. Michael would yell and scream at everybody. And one day Michael told me that Bill said to him, " 'If you yell and scream at me again I'm gonna kick your ass.' " When I got to Auburn I was an eighteen-year-old kid who was basically lazy. And my head coach, Sonny Smith, would tell me over and over, "Charles, you're fat and lazy." And I'm thinking, "If I'm leading the Southeastern Conference in rebounding, these other guys must really be lazy." So Sonny and I were always butting heads, and after two years I was just ready to leave. But one night we sat down and had dinner and I told him, "Sonny, if you change your approach just a little . . ." And after that he said to me once, "Charles, you're doing great . . . now if we could just do this a little better," and it made all the difference in the world in my case. Leading a team is difficult: it's so much about knowing when to do something and when not to.

I've got to tell this story about some of the best basketball advice I ever got. People looking in from the outside think that the most important thing is Xs and Os and devising strategies for certain situations. And yeah, that stuff is damn important at the end of games and in special situations. But when I first got to Auburn, Roger Banks watched me struggle with rebounding and he told me, "Son, you averaged twenty rebounds a game in high school . . . I'm gonna watch you for a while and figure out why you're not rebounding here." He came back to me after watching me and said, "No wonder you're not rebounding; quit boxing out and go after the damn ball." I'm standing there looking at him . . . he just told me the opposite of what people preach all the time and he said, "Son, go get the ball. If you're blocking out all the time, five rebounds might bounce right to you, but we didn't bring you here to get five rebounds a game." So much for conventional methods. Might be the best basketball advice I ever got. I'm so glad Roger took me under his wing from Day 1 at Auburn.

I guess the thing I'd want any young or aspiring player to take away from this is that making a successful career in anything has to do with so much more than pure talent. And that doesn't pertain to just sports. I'd bet it's the same way with any profession. It's just that sports are right out there in the open for everybody to see. But there's a lot of talent wasted in the world because people don't realize that what's just as important as the physical skills and the Xs and Os— maybe more important—is managing your life and staying away from the big mistakes that can ruin your career, ruin your life no matter how much talent you have.

If the Playing Is All You're Going to Do, You've Missed the Boat

I was watching a Bryant Gumbel *Real Sports* episode last summer that had a long segment on Muhammad Ali. And it was wonderful to see that his mind was so great. The guy reporting the piece reminded Ali that thirty-five years ago he had talked about the "white devil" and Ali said, "Hey, I was wrong, because the devil comes in various colors and it has nothing to do with race or ethnicity." While he doesn't sound like the old Ali and it's painful to see him suffering from Parkinson's disease, his mind is still very sharp. It's still Ali's mind and it just makes you feel better to see that that's the case. I met Ali once, in 1996 at the Atlanta Olympics. I walked up to him and said, "I'm so pleased to meet you. You're probably the greatest influence in my life." And he said, "Aaaaaw, I'm just another nigga." He was a great influence on my life because of the hope he'd given black people in the 1960s and '70s, and the way we felt so proud not just because of the great fights he won and the great skill he displayed, but because of the way he put himself out there when doing so could cost a black person his career, his wealth, and his freedom.

I guess what I'm getting at is, Ali's boxing career has been over for twenty-five years, really, and he still has worldwide impact. He didn't stop using his influence when he stopped boxing. Retirement may be the end of your athletic career, it's the end of physical influence in the arena of competition. But it's just the start of your adult life. And I guess I'm paying real close attention to all this stuff even more now that I'm new to retirement and trying to figure how best to use the influence that comes with playing in the NBA for sixteen years and making money and building relationships with other people who have money and influence.

What it amounts to is that God gave me some special stuff through basketball, and it just seems like a waste if I don't do something more than play golf and count my money. Ali stepped out there, man. Refusing to go in the Army and being the first public person of great stature to oppose the Vietnam War so openly, embracing Islam, Ali put it way out there. As historic a figure as Jackie Robinson is, Branch Rickey had to find someone with the necessary demeanor for dealing with all the ugly racist behavior that was going to come his way. But Ali, you had to take him as he was. And even then he lost the three most prime years of his career. I mean, at some point standing for something important is what defines you, even beyond athletic achievement. John Carlos and Tommie Smith could have kept quiet and done nothing on that medal stand in 1968 in Mexico City. But because they gave that gloved salute, there was no celebration for them when they got back to the U.S. Curt Flood was pushed away forever from baseball. No TV career, no coaching, no front office, just blackballed. He could have ridden the gravy train forever if he'd played along, but he didn't and now look what his sacrifice has done for major league ballplayers.

And those guys made significant contributions during their careers, which is even more amazing. So how can you not want to make some kind of contribution after your career? I just think if you are fortunate enough to have a productive career and you can put away some money and set yourself up, you have an obligation in your next career to do something meaningful. It doesn't have to be in the public spotlight, it just needs to be something that can make a difference. Things have gotten a lot better for athletes and entertainers who are black, but not for regular black folks. When it's over and you don't have any money and you've squandered your influence, that's just sad to me. I don't know whether to be mad at the Darryl Strawberrys, the Dwight Goodens and the Mike Tysons or feel sorry for them. Mike Tyson has made HBO and Don King and all those leeches millions and millions of dollars. And for him to have no money or even a tiny fraction of what he made, it's just unthinkable. Black and Hispanic communities don't have so many people of wealth and influence that we can lose any.

I'll bet you Earvin Johnson is getting more satisfaction from the impact he's having as an entrepreneur in his second career than he did in his first. I know people will read this and think, "Oh, Charles is crazy," but I'm serious about this. Don't get me wrong, a lot of people got great joy from Magic Johnson's basketball career, the way he ran the Lakers' "Showtime" and entertained people and played some of the best basketball ever. But from being around him some during his retirement, I really believe he's getting more enjoyment from his entrepreneurial efforts. It's so profoundly significant what he's doing. He's creating revenue, creating jobs for people in communities that go years without seeing new businesses of that magnitude come into the neighborhood. And it's not just revenue for himself he's creating; he's bringing people along. Earvin is improving people's lives. Seriously, how cool is that?

Earvin found something great in retirement that he's passionate about and good at and he's making a huge contribution. It's not easy finding the right fit when you retire from something so high-profile and financially rewarding when you're still in your thirties. It's very difficult because the first thing you have to do is be honest with yourself and most guys aren't honest with themselves. First thing is you're not going to work a nine-to-five job. Guys making the minimum are getting $1 million for playing basketball, so there's almost no chance you're going to a nine-to-five job, make $60,000 and be passionate about whatever it is.

You've got to convince yourself, "I've had the greatest time of my life playing pro basketball. It's never going to be more exciting or more glamorous than it was when I was playing, so let's get on with the next phase of life." Then you have to realize you're going to get bored just playing golf every day. Then, with the help of people you trust and whose advice you value, you have to try to figure out what it is you're good at and what it is you want to do with the rest of your life.

I'm thirty-nine years old and I've never had a real job.

I played organized basketball from nine until thirty-seven. That qualifies as my whole damn life.

Even before the leg injury in my last year, I said to myself, "I don't want to play like this." Yeah, I could have played two or three more years on my name. But I knew I was too good to play the way I was playing. Later in my career, I was playing all right, but just all right. I watch Hakeem Olajuwon and Patrick Ewing play now: both of those guys are right at forty, and I hate watching them play. I hate watching Michael play now. I say that because these guys playing now couldn't have stayed on the court with Hakeem and Patrick and Michael ten years ago, and I love those guys.

Even before the injury I suffered at the start of the 2000 season, I'd already announced I was going to retire. The Rockets had promised they were going to pay me $12 million, then changed it to $9 million as we got closer to the season. As long as I'd been in the NBA, teams had done under-the-table deals with players, and I vehemently disagree with the league's punishment of the Timberwolves for a practice that's common around the league. I wasn't going to play. But six weeks before the start of the season, I said, "Well, the NBA has been great to me. I could bitch about this, but I've had it too good—I'm going to go ahead and play." So I was twenty pounds overweight when the season began and that's probably why I got hurt.

The thing I was thinking was, "Man, I got carried off the court in my last game. I've got to go out there and try to play again." So I did. I just felt I needed to walk off the court for the final time. So I did the rehab and came back for that one more game. Rudy Tomjanovich said, "Get a rebound and score a basket." And the funny thing was, I went up and down the court ten times and couldn't get near the ball. I meant to jump five times and the ball was still a week away. I wanted to jump, it just wasn't there. I would look at the rebound coming and think, "Shit, that ball is a long way away."

Anyway, the last basket of my career was an offensive rebound basket, which was fitting.

The only part I miss is the basketball. The stuff that goes along with it, I don't miss. It wasn't easy, getting past ball. And when Michael called and said, "I want you to come back," you gotta say to yourself, "Damn. He thinks enough of me to ask me to come back with him." You walk around puffing your chest out for a few days because it sounds like a good idea at the time. But a professional athlete knows his body. I've said it before but I'll say it again: Michael was getting in shape but all I was getting was tired. You come to the realization, "I'm almost forty years old; this ain't workin.'" If the Greatest Ever's body breaks down, mine sure as hell would have broken down. Michael's got highway miles on him; I've got off-road miles.

It's a difficult transition. People wonder, "Why can't these guys stay out of trouble?" It's harder than you think it is. You've gotten spoiled and relatively lazy. You've got twenty-four hours a day with nothing to do and money to get into stuff you shouldn't. How many second careers are there that most guys can do beyond going into TV, coaching or working in the front office of an organization? I wonder how many guys have their degrees when they retire. I wish there was a study to consult about the percentage of guys who do. I didn't complete my degree at Auburn. I went back the first couple of summers; I had promised my grandmother I'd graduate. But I was making $1 million a year early in my career, and I wound up obviously making a lot more than that. If I'd needed to go back and graduate, I would have, but I didn't. Of course economics are a consideration. If you don't have access to that kind of wealth you'd better have more formal education and you'd better have your degree.

Economic considerations determine so much of what guys pursue for a second career, and whether they do something they really want or do something just because they need the money. Take that Fox *Celebrity Boxing.* How sad was that? I only watched to see Manute Bol. First of all, how much are the celebrity boxers getting paid? We know Fox is getting paid because the show had a huge prime-time rating. But you don't participate in stuff like that unless you need the money. It's so sad to retire and need money that badly, although Manute's case is a little different because of the charities he was heavily involved in.

And "Refrigerator" Perry was pretty much as big as it got in the mid-1980s. He had to make a little money during that period. But here he is in this *Celebrity Boxing*. And let me tell you who's really pathetic: Darva Conger. She does that stupid Fox marry-a-millionaire show where she marries that clown, then when the whole world is talking about it–like she didn't know what she was doing when she signed up for it–she says, "Oh, I've made a big mistake here, and all I want to do is go back to my private life and be left alone."

I was feeling for her a little bit. Public life can be hell, especially when you go from nobody knowing who you are to everybody getting into every aspect of your life. So I'm thinking, "Okay, anybody can make a mistake and if all she wants is her private life back, we ought to cut her some slack and let her do that." Next thing you know, she's posing for *Playboy* magazine, and I'm thinking, "Oh, this is how you go about getting your private life back?" Now, she's on in prime time in *Celebrity Boxing*? Come on now. I guess she didn't exactly want that private life back, did she? Darva being on it is bad enough, but to see Manute and the Fridge . . . I'm telling you, it's difficult. You're in your late thirties, early forties, and you just can't play golf every day and sit around. But on the other hand, there's got to be a plan and you have to be honest with yourself. What really helps is to be around somebody who goes about it the right way when you're young so you can get some idea of what the hell is going on.

You know who really prepared me for retirement? Julius Erving and Moses Malone. And I was twenty-one years old when I met 'em. I was fortunate because Doc has a great sense of business and Moses is so streetwise. Doc was starting his transition from playing to retirement when I first got to Philly. Those guys were a fountain of information. And I'm fortunate to have been able to pick their brains, and that they were so free with their time and their advice. I'll tell you one thing that bothered me a little bit at the end of my career. I knew my body was breaking down and I couldn't play the way I used to, and I thought one of the ways I could contribute to the league was to help some of the young guys. It's only right, since I had benefited from the advice of veterans, to be there for a new generation of young guys. I looked forward to it, to tell you the truth. But when I tried to be there for 'em, their attitude was like, "Hey old man, sit your ass down somewhere over there. You're trying to hold us back." And you just kind of sit there and say to yourself, "Can you believe this shit?" It's not just me either. I've talked to other guys near retirement and they've had similar stories to tell.

I guess I just want guys never ever to take for granted how unbelievable our lives are, how much influence we have and how much impact we can have. Man, I want to see guys maximize their impact after athletics, not throw it away while they're still playing on entourages and silly crap. So my story isn't complete yet. In ten to fifteen years, if I've helped some struggling people build something good, then it'll be a complete story.

To me, this is all connected if you want to try to fight poverty and illiteracy and racism. The legacy of slavery is that nothing was passed down. We're still at the point where a successful black person is taking care of, or at least helping out, the previous generation in his family, instead of the other way around. You ain't got many black kids having college paid for by a trust fund. We still don't own much of anything. Most of the blacks who are successful don't own stuff. It's athletes and celebrities. We're not able to provide an economic path for the next generation.

Just look at a few examples in sports. Jerry Colangelo, the owner of the Phoenix Suns and Arizona Diamondbacks, brought his son Bryan aboard years ago. Jerry is the CEO of the Suns, Bryan is the president of the organization. I'm not trying to accuse Jerry of nepotism. But it's just like Jeremy Schaap coming into broadcasting largely because of his late father, Dick. Or it's like Joe Buck following Jack Buck or Chip Caray following his father, Skip Caray, and both of them following Chip's grandfather and Skip's father, Harry. It's the family business. Even if they don't own it, they own a stake in it. I love working with Ernie Johnson, Jr., who's a damn hardworking guy, and he would be the first to tell you how much he owed his father, Ernie Johnson, Sr., who was the broadcast voice of the Atlanta Braves for so long. With damn few exceptions, black folks don't have that in industries that produce wealth or ownership. It wasn't until I was playing for the Olympic team and met Bishop Desmond Tutu that I even considered the impact I might have overseas because of my athletic career. It didn't really cross my mind until he brought these little South African kids wearing our basketball jerseys telling us that there were no black men in positions of huge influence where they live.

So, as much as it pained me to watch Ali get beat like he did in his last few fights, it's not the sports stuff that matters as much in the end. There will always be great players here and there, in this sport or that sport. And we all love seeing that and celebrating it and debating it. But those of us who were given these great talents and unique gifts by God have to speak up and put it out there, even if it isn't popular, even if it isn't politically correct all the time. If the playing is all you're going to do, you've missed the boat. I may be wrong, but I doubt it.

About the Authors

Charles Barkley is a studio analyst for TNT's *Inside the NBA,* a regular contributor to CNN's *TalkBack Live* and a frequent color commentator. Named one of the fifty greatest NBA players of all time, he was selected to eleven All-Star teams and won the NBA's MVP award in 1993. He lives in Scottsdale, Arizona.

Michael Wilbon is a *Washington Post* sports columnist and the cohost, with Tony Kornheiser, of the ESPN show *Pardon the Interruption.* He lives outside Washington, D.C.

About the Type

This book was set in Walbaum, a typeface designed in 1810 by German punch cutter J. E. Walbaum. Walbaum's type is more French than German in appearance. Like Bodoni, it is a classical typeface, yet its openness and slight irregularities give it a human, romantic quality.